WINNING THE NEGOTIATION

Winning the Negotiation

Negotiation

HENRY H. CALERO

HAWTHORN BOOKS, INC.
Publishers/NEW YORK
A Howard & Wyndham Company

WINNING THE NEGOTIATION

Library of Congress Catalog Card Number: 79-84208

ISBN:0-8015-3680-4

10 9 8 7 6 5 4 3 2 1

This book is dedicated to my brothers and sisters, Frank, Jimmy, Manuel, Hope, Bea, Joe, and Richard, who unknowingly taught me how to negotiate successfully at an early age.

Contents

Introduction   ix
Negotiating Skills Questionnaire   xii
1 It Starts in the Cradle   1
2 What Is Negotiation?   22
3 The Negotiating Ritual   38
4 The 1962 Cuban Missile Crisis:
   A Case Study in Negotiation   66
5 Mistakes Committed by Negotiators   76
6 Alternatives at an Impasse   94
7 Strategy and Tactics   106
8 Planning Your Next Negotiation   121
9 Developing Your Negotiating Skills   138
10 Profile Questionnaire Response   154
   Index   172

Introduction

A father took his six-year-old daughter for a short walk one day and as they passed a toy store she stopped to look at the window display. "Daddy," she said, "please buy me that toy." Her father replied: "I don't have any money with me"—to which she quickly responded, "That's OK, write a check." When he answered, "I didn't bring my checkbook with me," she emphatically retorted, "Then charge it."

The outcome of this story is very clear to any parent who has ever been or will be outnegotiated by a child. That six-year-old child negotiated successfully because she applied two very important principles of negotiating. First, she was persistent and would not accept no for an answer; second, she exercised alternatives and gave her father other options that satisfied her needs. These two factors—persistence and the generation of alternatives—

along with other elements of negotiating, are the subject of this book.

I have spent fourteen years researching the subject of negotiating and have recorded several thousand role-playing sessions on videotape for many U.S. corporations. In addition, I have conducted executive seminars for thousands of businessmen in the United States, Canada, Mexico, Europe, and Australia. My objective has been to understand the dynamics of a process that is essentially paradoxical. Negotiation is both simple and complex: common to all human beings yet little understood; very personal among individuals yet often totally impersonal between groups; highly emotional at times and analytical at others; competitive while being supportive. Although sometimes very frustrating, negotiation is also one of the most rewarding experiences when we are successful. Furthermore, there is a great deal of acting involved by many participants who are deadly serious. The process is very intuitive yet pragmatic; some play it as they would a structured game and lose while winning. It is a process that—even when skillfully handled—is constantly on the verge of catastrophe and breakdown. Finally, negotiation is an involvement we cannot escape, regardless of age, culture, social position, or occupation.

The irony is that very little research has been done in the field of negotiation—universities and colleges seldom offer courses on the subject. Strange indeed that one of man's most important skills for survival is so little understood.

The objective of this book is to look at the process

and dynamics involved; to observe the most fundamental elements and see what happens; to understand why we succeed and fail; to improve our skills in everyday negotiations; to increase our self-knowledge and thereby handle conflict and stressful situations more effectively. In summary, the aim of this book is to enable successful management of a negotiating situation so that both parties have a mutual feeling of "I gave but also I got."

A crucial distinction made herein is the difference between negotiation and confrontation. Not recognizing the difference between the two is one of the main reasons for unsuccessful negotiations. Only when we clearly understand the difference can we consciously decide which of the two processes to use.

Become involved with this book; try to sense the stressful flavor of each situation. Make an initial commitment by taking a self-inventory before reading the text. Use the questionnaire that follows to assess your own responses. (The final chapter will discuss and analyze the results.)

NEGOTIATING SKILLS QUESTIONNAIRE

	Almost Never	Seldom	Sometimes	Often	Almost Always
1. When people disagree with your views or position, do you try to convince them?					
2. When conflict exists between two parties, do you feel like compromising in order to resolve the dispute?					
3. Do you believe that your usual preparations for a negotiation are adequate?					
4. Do you believe that the person with the most facts will eventually be successful in a negotiation?					
5. Once you have decided what your objectives are, do you change them during the course of negotiating?					
6. Is it possible for both parties in a negotiation to win?					
7. Do individuals who negotiate play games?					
8. Do these games negatively influence the negotiation?					
9. When your opponent's strategy is to play games with you, do you counter with your own games?					
10. Do you prepare written questions before negotiating?					
11. Do your questions cause anxiety when asked?					
12. Is the person asking the most questions in control?					
13. Can a caucus or adjournment be taken as a weakness?					
14. Is a caucus an effective procedure?					

	Almost Never	Seldom	Sometimes	Often	Almost Always
15. Should illogical approaches be used?					
16. Does losing your temper negatively influence the negotiation?					
17. When reaching an impasse, is it better to call the negotiation to a halt and leave?					
18. Should the first and/or final offer be made by your opponent?					
19. Do most individuals *know* when it is time to close a deal or end a negotiation?					
20. Can negotiators read each other "like a book"?					
21. Is it true that the more dominant a negotiator is, the more effective he becomes?					
22. Does the supportive negotiator tend to experience less conflict in negotiations?					
23. Is the use of levity effective?					
24. Should compliments be used?					
25. Should opening statements and positions be emphatic?					
26. Does the amount of time spent in negotiating influence the outcome?					
27. Do most negotiators enjoy stressful periods?					
28. Is it easier to negotiate on the telephone?					
29. When individuals say "That's not negotiable," should you believe them?					
30. Are additional team negotiating members useful?					

	Almost Never	Seldom	Sometimes	Often	Almost Always
31. Should the "hard-nosed" approach be used?					
32. Is negotiating in your office an advantage to you?					
33. Are negotiators truthful about what they "want"?					
34. Do most negotiators listen?					
35. When individuals "walk out" of a negotiation, is it planned?					
36. In general, are negotiators very creative?					

WINNING THE NEGOTIATION

1

It Starts in the Cradle

As early as the cradle, we start negotiating for simple needs—love, caressing, food. Later in life, we continue to negotiate—for attention, recognition, and love. In childhood our objectives depend to a great extent on our survival needs. In adult life they depend more on psychological needs.

We begin to develop our negotiating skills at an early age, quickly finding that crying gets attention, and we learn to use it to satisfy our needs. Occasionally, crying doesn't work and individuals ignore us, so we add rattling the bars of our crib to our repertoire of tactics. We soon learn that others pay attention to us when we smile, so we smile a lot—and continue to cry a great deal and make noise. These are our early negotiating tactics. Some adult negotiators still use them; we refer to such people as "crib-type" negotiators.

Since, during infancy, verbal communication is not yet possible, we continue to develop and add to our nonverbal messages that say, "I want," "You please me," "Play with me," "Stroke me"—all "I-oriented" messages. At this point, we are strictly negotiating from the *get* point of view, and anything we *give* is purely accidental, for we don't think about what our parents want or need. Thus in this phase of the negotiating situation the child is *get*-oriented and the parents *give*-oriented. Later in life, as we shall see, these roles have to be reversed if we are to be successful.

Self-deprivation and self-injury constitute the next level of negotiating we discover. By holding our breath, refusing to eat, banging our heads, biting ourselves, etc., we sometimes get others to do our bidding and satisfy our needs. An interesting turnabout occurs when the infant negotiates for its physical needs by actions that tend to harm it physically.

We move from this phase quickly and discover another strategy—*not* returning any smiles, *not* giving any affection to the parent. This is the "I don't love you anymore" phase, which we never entirely forget, and utilize from time to time throughout the rest of our lives.

Somewhere between the ages of four and ten the child discovers the tactic of *stroke-and-get*. We become aware that a little bit of sugar (compliment) may yield many rewards in return. The child who says to her father, "Daddy, that's a nice suit you bought; you look so handsome," and follows it with "May I have a dollar?" has learned this negotiating ploy and may use it at every possible opportunity. Girls usually reach this stage sooner than boys, possibly because little boys are normally given such things as trucks, balls, or guns to play with while girls are given dolls, which for them become mirror images of life and real people. As a result, little girls learn earlier the effectiveness of giving a compliment, while little boys tend still to be locked into the "I want" phase and must get before they give. Sometimes boys will realize the value of the "give" gambit after observing how successful their sister or mother is with that strategy.

WHY CHILDREN ARE SUCCESSFUL NEGOTIATORS

When my seminar attendees are asked why their children are successful as negotiators, the responses usually are these: (1) because they are persistent; (2) they can read me like a book; (3) they are uninhibited; (4) they know what they want; (5) they know when to ask for what they want (timing); (6) they know how to divide parents to get what they want from the more compromising one; (7) they are honest in their demands; (8) they are very creative in their approaches.

An analysis of these eight reasons will reveal many characteristics of the successful child-negotiator that continue into adulthood. Let's begin with the last and work backward.

Creative Alternatives

Children are extremely creative in developing alternatives. They start with *why* and *why not* and believe that anything is possible. A particularly burning question in their minds seems to be *how*. And the need for answers to these questions prompts originality. In addition, children have not yet developed a strong logical approach to thinking so they use what Edward de Bono calls *lateral thinking*. Take as an example the story of a six-year-old who helped solve a freeway tieup in Los Angeles.

A truck carrying a heavy load of hay was wedged in an underpass because of the low clearance. Policemen, motorists, and the truck driver were in a quandary as to how to free the truck. The alternatives being discussed were: shifting the load of hay; setting fire to the top of the hay and standing by with water hoses; stopping auto traffic on the bridge and removing a section of it. The young boy watching all the action kept yelling something to the men. Finally, one of the policemen listened to him. His suggestion? "Let the air out of the tires."

While in New York City one hot summer day, I dreaded the prospect of riding a subway car without air conditioning. A friend of mine—a very successful engineer—remarked: "Not to worry." Apparently he knew each car and the equipment it carried and would select the car with air conditioning before we got on. A boy no more than seven years old heard our intelligent conversation and shot us down by saying: "I know an easier way. I look to see which cars have closed windows."

Children tend to be extremely creative.

Honesty

Give or take a nefarious youngster or two, most children approach their parents with straightforward, sincere, and honest demands, needs, or conditions. For the most part, children are "up front" with their needs. Such an approach can be disarming to a parent who is sometimes conditioned to tactics that are more secretive, manipulative, and self-serving. Further, because we tend to admire honesty and integrity and want these characteristics in our children, using them can be to the child's advantage. The oft-told George Washington story is a good example. (The part of the story that has always puzzled me is why George's father asked him if he chopped down the tree but never asked him why.)

Many parents are completely caught off guard when approached by a child who say, "I know you are not going to like what I'm going to tell you," meaning bad news will follow; or, "I hope you will help me in a serious problem." What often motivates children here is the parents' offer: "Let me know when you need help or are in trouble"—an offer children may take as carte blanche to get them off the hook in any difficult situation. The children disarm parents with an apparent honesty that gets the parent to shoulder a problem. In this negotiating situation parents might be more effective if they were to use the "help yourself" tactic and respond, "What are you going to do about it?" This would allow their offspring to develop alternatives and courses of action of their own rather than give them set answers and solutions.

Divide and Conquer

Wise parents do not allow a child to use the divide-and-conquer tactic to outnegotiate them. However, many of us quickly fall for this ploy and find ourselves no longer negotiating with the child but with our spouse. This is an approach that works especially well when both parents are trying hard to become the child's friend. The child is able to test which parent is going to be more difficult and determined. Once having used this tactic successfully, the child files it away for future use—it surfaces in many an adult negotiator. The difficulty occurs when the strategy is used too often. It can then prove counterproductive. Children, as well as adult negotiators, have a tendency to abuse successful techniques to the point where they eventually elicit negative results.

A five-year-old asked his mother for a bicycle and she said no. "OK," he responded, "let's go in the bedroom and play mommy and daddy." She was so shocked that she didn't answer. The next day the boy again asked for a bike and again received a rejection, and again he said, "OK, let's play mommy and daddy." The third day he once more asked for the bicycle. In desperation his mother finally agreed to play mommy and daddy. In the bedroom her son went to his father's clothes closet, pulled out a shirt, tie, and coat, put them on and then patted his mother softly on the arm and said, "That's a good girl now, give the boy his bicycle." The son had evidently observed that he could manipulate his mother through his father.

Timing

Children seem to possess an extraordinary ability to know when to ask for something. How beneficial it would be if we could all sharpen our timing skills to a higher degree! Children have a delicate sense of timing—in the way that Jack Benny had it for humor—an uncanny awareness of when to ask for money, clothes, or that bicycle.

A father once questioned his four-year-old son about why he waited until either before or after the first of each month to ask for things that cost money. He thought it was unusual since the child could not read the calendar. The child replied, "I never ask you for things that cost money when you get all those letters with the funny windows on them." The boy had observed that when bills were received in the mail, it was not the time to ask for items that cost money.

A seminar attendee told me that his eight-year-old daughter always knew when to ask for things. She waited for those peak moments in marriage when all seemed to be going well and would then say to him: "Daddy, I hope that when I get married I find someone just like you." Then *zap* with the request. Under such circumstances, who could say no?

Knowing What They Want

When children have their minds set on something, they seldom settle for substitutes. When I was a youngster, I recall wanting a recording of "Chattanooga Choo Choo" by the great Glenn Miller band. After telling my mother about my wish for several weeks, she finally bought the record. The problem was that the record was made by some other band. It didn't sound like Glenn Miller's version and was shorter in playing time. I tried to hide my disappointment from my mother, although I'm sure she saw through me. Nonetheless, I kept the recording and looked forward to the day that I would have the Miller recording. Then Raymond, a friend of mine, told me about an uncle who collected records. I asked Raymond if his uncle had my record of "Chattanooga Choo Choo" and he said no. A negotiation followed in which I sold Raymond's uncle my record for enough money to buy the record I wanted. After I'd played the record incessantly for a month, my mother casually asked if that was the recording she had bought for me. I told her it was but she probably knew the truth.

You can probably identify with the foregoing or recall many situations in which children have been unwilling to settle for less. In this regard, children sometimes exercise higher levels of expectation than they do as adults. For every adult who aspires to become president of the United States, I'll wager there are thousands of children who have their eyes set on that office. As will be evident further on, setting high goals is important for successful negotiating.

Uninhibited

Society, it has been said, shapes our behavior. The child negotiator apparently hasn't reached a point where he is easily influenced by the customs and standards of society. As a result, the behavior towards parent and others is "let it all hang out." Children cry very easily without attempting to hide hurt and tears; they become angry suddenly; they don't say, "Everything's all right" when it isn't. When children dislike you, it is very apparent and they don't do much to cover up animosity. This lack of inhibition has two advantages: It allows for a greater potential creativity, and it also finds the child ready to use whatever tactic is most effective to get him what he wants. Of course, this trait is not always easy for adults to employ or adopt.

They Can Read You

Have you ever convinced a child that you liked him when you didn't? A friend tells me his four-year-old grandniece, whom he dislikes very much, refers to him as "that man" instead of uncle. His nephew has made repeated attempts to get her to call him "uncle," without success. The little girl has read the nonverbal messages well and her reaction is, "I don't like you." In general, children read adults better than adults read children. Similarly, women read men better than men read women.

The intuitive ability to read others—to receive friend-or-foe messages—is an important survival skill developed in youth. Observe the approach of two young children who are strangers to each other. They stare and watch for any telltale nonverbal clue that might indicate friendliness, fear, or hostility. Narrowing the distance between them is similar to the ritual of two young animals. Moreover, since a child's survival depends on his or her parents, it is not surprising that the youngster reads the meal ticket so well.

Children start reading consistency into their parents'

behavior patterns as a means of adjusting to their environment. Thus a child can very easily tolerate a chronically bad-tempered father because the irritated or angry reaction is familiar. The child is confused only when the parent does not react as expected. Ask five-year-old children to describe their parents' daily routines and they will amaze you with a welter of detailed information. A child may even reveal that his father puts on his left shoe before the right one when dressing.

If I were to write a detective story I'd have a youngster as one of my central characters. This child would observe, in the manner of a young Miss Marple, many things that would seem to be unimportant but, when put together, would provide a telling clue. Many successful negotiators similarly observe the most minute clues about another negotiator, file their observations away, and use them in the future.

Persistence

Most parents would agree that children are persistent in their demands, for when wants are not fulfilled, they usually keep trying. And I don't know of a single successful negotiator who is not persistent. The ability to continue trying without giving up or admitting defeat has made some men giants in the eyes of historians. What is the strong force that underlies such stamina? Optimism, I believe, is at the root of persistence. If a person is not optimistic about achieving, overcoming difficulty, or succeeding, that person probably will not persevere. I have two favorite optimist stories. The first is that of the seventy-two-year-old man who married a twenty-two-year-old woman and then bought a five-bedroom home next door to a grammar school; the second is that of a woman of ninety-two who told me how proud she was of a pair of gloves she had recently purchased. It seems that the gloves were guaranteed against wearing out for two years. She will, it is hoped, still be using those gloves on her ninety-fourth birthday.

Children, as well as successful negotiators, do not take no to be final. To them it means "maybe." Consider the newspaper report of a child of six who insisted that his lost dog would be found. Despite three months of searching and many offers of rewards that proved futile, the child refused to stop searching. Then one day, while on vacation several hundred miles away, the family saw the dog in the back of a pickup truck. The new owners, after much questioning, finally admitted that the dog had been taken as a stray several months ago. The child exclaimed to the dog, "I knew we would find you."

Although success has been described in many ways, the ability to persist and continue to try seems to be common to all success stories. How many businessmen do you know who were successful in their first venture? Ask Ray Kroc of McDonald's about that and he will tell you how many times he failed in other fields.

WHEN YOUNGSTERS CEASE NEGOTIATING AND START DEMANDING

Adolescents, while expressing the duality of self-reliance and dependency, apparently forget all the aspects of negotiating that were developed in early childhood, and return to the "demand" strategy of infancy, but with a different vehemency. This technique is not very successful except with parents who enjoy being intimidated by their children. A child psychologist once remarked about adolescent children, "They have all the weapons." My response to him was, "Who put them in their hands?" Hence at the adolescent stage of life, negotiating skills sink to their lowest. The "I" orientation returns to the adolescent; the stroking of parents, used successfully earlier in life, is forgotten. Fortunately for all concerned, these tendencies soften as adolescents come to recognize that intimidation is not successful in the long run.

Intimidation

Intimidation has worked, is working, and will work as a negotiating tactic for a short period, but seldom for a long one. The most intimidating of governments, leaders, and rulers eventually must learn this vital lesson to stay in power. However, for some reason, adolescent youngsters have a very difficult time understanding this lesson, so our negotiations with them often break down. They rebel—run away (walk out), quit school, accept fads, and so forth. In general, we often reach an impasse. Our daily newspapers are filled with examples that reflect a breakdown in the give-and-take that makes up negotiation in the family. My belief is that this is the most dangerous period in our lives, for both the adolescents and the parents. However, it does pass, and the experi-

ence aids us in our ability to negotiate effectively for
the rest of our lives.

Adolescents—and adults—must acquire a long-term
view of a situation rather than succumb to short-term
ego needs to be "right" or to "teach someone a lesson."
Also in this negotiating period, adolescents don't necessarily go for *get* objectives but for *prove* objectives—to
prove that someone is wrong, old fashioned, not with it,
or foolish. This is frequently true of parents as well.
Young children are more interested in getting things.
While this motive never completely disappears, in the
movement to adulthood we see that people increasingly
feel compelled to prove things.

One of the most frequently asked questions at seminars is how to negotiate with individuals who are considerably older. People usually seem to think this is a
very difficult situation. I surprise the questioners by
saying, "You're in heaven and don't know it." My response is based on the awareness that most human
beings over the age of thirty-five have a strong propen-
sity to tell someone younger what they have learned or
experienced in life. Therefore, if a younger person uses a
pupil-to-mentor approach for purposes of picking up
possible information, the older participant tends to be
very kind and considerate. However, when the pupil
tells the mentor that everything the latter believes is no
longer valid or useful (intimidation), then the mentor
becomes an enemy.

Parents often don't help their own negotiating position. They are too frequently *because*-oriented, and
attempt to get the opponent (adolescent) to do their

bidding "because this," "because that," instead of seeking alternatives or negotiating. They are, in effect, behaving just like their demanding adolescent. Two parties behaving in the same way and using similar tactics eventually reach an impasse. Resolution has a better chance if the parties do not behave in the same manner. The next time you have one of those heated "I'm right, you're wrong" arguments with your teenager, think about what other alternatives you can exercise.

MOVING INTO MATURITY

On the way to adulthood, we should acquire certain basic approaches to dealing with others, approaches that are as important to the negotiating process as they are to being mature.

Either/Or, Instead of If/Then

Few negotiators ever enter into negotiations with the idea of not succeeding—yet the percentage of unintentional failures is amazing. One of the major reasons for failure is that we inadvertently create *either/or* situations instead of *if/then* situations. I learned of this difference early in my business career during my own Young Turk phase, that period when one is itching for a chance to prove oneself. I had been asking for and got a responsible assignment, which in time I was able to handle efficiently. The difficulty was that monetary rewards did not come along as soon as I had anticipated. One day I decided to raise the issue with my boss. I told him, "Either I get more money or I leave." He wisely responded, "If you leave, then . . ." and mentioned other alternatives that I had not considered. He made me aware of the inflexible position I had taken, which caused me to appear unwilling to negotiate. Our meeting ended when he said, "I'll see what I can do about a raise." A week later I received more than usual in my paycheck and my supervisor's comment was, "Hank, you got away with it this time. Remember you may not be as fortunate the next time." My boss clearly recognized my either/or approach and softened it to an if/then situation that allowed for negotiation.

Many people do not understand the difference between confrontation (either/or) and negotiation (if/then). It is much easier to move from negotiation to confrontation than the reverse. Beginning a negotiation session with an either/or confrontation usually hardens the opponent's stance.

Some seminar attendees, however, have questioned whether the either/or position used initially cannot later be softened to an if/then, thus leading to a successful negotiation. I do believe that initial either/or positions can lead to settlements, but usually when both parties are aware of the ritual involved and the words are discounted to mean, "We're opening hard and softening later." It is the same when no is taken as meaning maybe and maybe as meaning "yes, if you try harder."

Smoothing the Rough Edges

We enter maturity after much abrasive wear and tear. Almost inevitably we begin to show more adaptability when dealing with conflict. No longer do we tend to let our emotions rule us. We try to deal with problems by looking into and discovering what options or alternatives are available. Instead of reacting to stress instinctively, we tend to hold back angry words. I remember a very profound observation made by a colleague years ago. He said, "I can remember more things I've said and wished I hadn't than things I felt like saying and didn't."

We grow less dogmatic and self-projecting—more tolerant, some say, of others' needs. We somehow become aware that others feel, think, and act differently, and we try to bridge that difference for mutual gain. The "everyone should get something" feeling is more prevalent than the "I want" left over from childhood and adolescence. You can probably recall many situations in which you felt like strangling someone you liked but who nonetheless persisted in making life difficult for you. Yet despite that strong urge, you didn't wrap your fingers around an antagonist's throat, but managed to keep the relationship going until the crisis passed. And after differences are resolved, you are likely to be extremely pleased that you didn't deprive another person of his oxygen supply.

Although we still feel emotions as strongly as we did when younger, we negotiate in a different manner. In fact, the toughest negotiation we must face for the rest of our lives is that between our rational selves and our feelings. The awareness of self-negotiation for some, fortunately, comes early in life. However, for many of us it comes much later. This may explain why some individuals have such an extremely difficult time adjusting to external changes. It has been my observation that those who have negotiated well with themselves find change to be a challenge rather than a traumatic experience. The best example I can find is that of the person who, parachuted into a strange territory, within a period of two weeks feels as though he has lived there most of his life. Now that's adjustment!

Patience Is Frustration Under Control

The meaning of the word "patience" has amused me since I was a child. I can recall my older brothers and sisters describing me as "very patient," when in my mind I was thoroughly frustrated with what was going on around me. To this day, when we have family reunions, my brothers and sisters still reflect that I was "a very patient youngster," unaware of the level of frustration I suffered. Thus I call patience frustration under control. After passing through the cradle experience and adolescent rebellion, the mature adult arrives at the "I'm in charge" stage of life's negotiating experience. He takes responsibility for his actions when negotiating. The captain is in command and must act the part. It is now that we find that our ability to exercise patience under frustrating conditions is a very powerful force in negotiating.

Considering Alternatives

When we consider how many difficulties we've created, how many conflicts we've been involved in, how many differences we've resolved, we begin to realize how often we have negotiated in life, both unsuccessfully and successfully. How to negotiate in dire or traumatic living situations appears to be one of the major problems that faces us—and the educational system unfortunately does little to prepare us to cope with these negotiating dilemmas.

A diplomat or statesman confronted with a serious international situation may use a historical model to approach the problem. He considers background information relative to what occurred and the possibility of its recurrence. This serves as a guide to possible alternatives for dealing with the problem. Homework in this type of situation is vitally important. In another situation, a company executive planning an acquisition negotiation will spend hundreds of hours in researching financial statements, performance records, market trends, sales forecasts, and the like. Only after compiling such data and evaluating it, is the executive thoroughly prepared for the negotiations.

However, sometimes in business or personal situations we negotiate very weighty or sensitive issues with a minimum of preparation and little awareness of the options and alternatives available to us. Many critical personal relationships are jeopardized by failure to introduce a problem for negotiation in a manner conducive to resolution. Take the matter of communicating to a loved one that he or she has a serious drinking problem that is adversely affecting their lives. Often this is handled awkwardly, but negotiation can be initiated effectively by thinking through how to approach the problem and sensing the probable reaction of the individual involved.

Let's look at some possible tactics for presenting the message.

1) In the "I care" approach, you stress your love and support for the person before you tell him your view of the problem. Then you back off and let him tell you his opinion.

2) Using the "why don't you" overture, you either explicitly or implicitly chastise the person for his/her action or conduct. If not stated as a criticism, this can be issued as a directive, as in the song, "Why don't you do right, like some other men do."

3) There is the "I may be wrong" gambit, in which you minimize your certainty about the danger or importance of the problem in hopes that the core message will not be received too harshly.

4) You can use the "I have a friend" message, which masks the true identity of the person involved, in hopes that the person you're addressing will unscramble the message's content and identify himself as the star of the drama.

5) You can say, "I know something is wrong," and state what is happening, give examples, and draw a conclusion neatly wrapped for the person to accept. This approach may lead to serious arguments, because we often employ a logic unacceptable to the other party; rationalization may prevail and the person initiating the discussion may wind up angry and frustrated.

6) You can try the use of a third party in the "would you talk to" strategy. With this tactic, you enlist the aid of someone who is well liked and respected in hopes that the person will listen to your message as spoken by

another party. The problem with this approach is that another person's communication may not be exactly the same as yours. Also, you must wait to ask the third person, "What did he say?" and unless the session was tape recorded you probably never will know for certain what transpired.

7) The "I don't know what's wrong, but unless things change" ultimatum expresses the either/or tactic in no uncertain terms. The person utilizing this approach had better be prepared to be put to the test and plan what action to take if things do not change. Generally, people do not react favorably when they feel they are being forced to do something. Some people will simply say, "Do it" and sit back and wait for the result of their fait accompli (now it's your turn).

8) The "When are you . . . ?" inquiry stresses that you have been patiently waiting for the other person to become aware of the situation and do something about it. This implies that the individual is stupid, insensitive, unconcerned, while you are all-knowing and aware.

9) With the "silent treatment," you invariably elicit an "all right, what's the matter?" response from the other individual. Then be prepared to use another approach, because you still have to indicate what you see the problem to be.

10) You can try a "kill them with kindness" strategy, wherein you are overly concerned with the other's comfort and likes. As with the silent treatment eventually the individual asks, "OK, what do you want?" Be aware then that "Oh, nothing" is a poor response and only tends to aggravate the problem. But, as does

the silent treatment, this tactic eventually opens up communication.

11) It often is effective to recognize your own part in a problem affecting your relationship with the other person. This tends to be the least neurotic approach to use in dealing with a serious interpersonal difficulty. If you see that something is wrong with your partner, you should be prepared to acknowledge that something may also be wrong with you. You can offer to bring about changes in yourself, if possible, to improve the situation.

12) There is also the ploy of leaving messages around. You obtain articles from magazines or newspapers dealing with the problem in hopes the partner will read them.

There is no absolutely right or wrong approach. At best, we can weigh the relative merits of the situation and then evaluate what direction might prove successful. The benefit of reassessing our options and alternatives is that we are more readily able to change directions during the course of approaching the problem rather than trying a single approach, failing, and not knowing what to do next. Although a formal business negotiation may not lend itself to an application of these exact tactics, an awareness of a range of tactics always provides the negotiator an edge. And many of the ploys you might find yourself considering using during a "structured" negotiation session are not so far removed from those noted above.

2

What Is Negotiation?

Before going on to an analysis of negotiating tactics, we should identify some basic features of the process that remain the same whatever the form of negotiation.

Man tends to be a social yet solitary animal. He wants to satisfy his needs, yet knows he must also satisfy those of others to achieve his goals. At the root of *all* negotiations are needs. Negotiating, therefore, might be defined as a process of satisfying needs.

You have probably encountered a situation in which another person said to you, "Why should I?" or "I don't need you." Unless you could draw out a real need in the eyes of the other individual, you probably were hard pressed to get him to negotiate. A disparity or lack of needs puts a damper on getting others to negotiate.

Historically, individuals, groups, companies, organizations, and nations enter into negotiations because there are fundamental needs they seek to fulfill. They negotiate because they want something and see this as a possible way in which objectives may be achieved. When one side does not acknowledge needs, the other side has to show persuasively that such needs do exist and that there is great value in satisfying them. This persuasion is sometimes referred to as "selling."

Many of my seminar attendees have remarked that negotiating is basically selling, or that the two processes are inexorably tied together. My response is that the two processes are very similar and have many common elements. There are, however, some differences, which will be discussed in detail throughout this book. But for now let's say that negotiating is a process of satisfying needs and that a successful negotiator knows how to sell and/or create needs.

MAXIMIZING NEEDS

Once a need exists we seek to maximize our position to get as much as we possibly can. This calls for setting up high objectives, with fallback positions so as to end up somewhere near our midpoint expectation level. In most negotiations both parties spend a great deal of time arriving at what the midpoint range is. The following buyer-seller objectives serve as an illustration:

The seller is attempting to get the highest price for his product or service ($2,250), whereas the buyer's goal is to pay the least amount ($1,000). Their mutual objec-

	$1,000	$1,500	$2,000
	Min		Max
Buyer	X_____		_____X

	$1,250	$1,750	$2,250
Seller	X_____		_____X

tive is to arrive at a shaded area (between $1,500 and $1,750). Because many negotiations have extreme high and low positions, arriving at that midpoint is often a signal that positive results will follow. To flush out that all-important range of negotiation, you should test your opponent's position by saying "You've told me what you *want*, now what do you *need*?" Once the range is established, then the serious task of trade-off can begin. It amazes me how many still do not understand this and make the process more difficult by arguing from fixed extreme positions rather than developing a range. Consider the probable outcome of an argument in which each party feels itself to be absolutely right and the other absolutely wrong, instead of both being equally right and wrong, so as to arrive at a compromise somewhere in between.

PROVIDING LEVERAGE

The next element in the process of negotiating is providing yourself with leverage to achieve your needs. Remember the James Garner movie *Support Your Local*

Sheriff? An incident in that film simply illustrates this part of the process. The sheriff, who doesn't carry a gun, is faced with a very serious situation when an outlaw pulls out a six-shooter and aims it point-blank at him. The sheriff provides himself leverage here by sticking his index finger into the pistol barrel and reminding the outlaw what happens to a person who has a jammed gun explode in his face. Both sheriff and outlaw walk away pleased that they didn't explore the outcome any further.

Another example is that of the woman going to the dentist to have a tooth filled. She is aware of the discomfort and pain normally involved in such a visit. To improve her position, as the dentist starts drilling she seizes the dentist in a sensitive spot below the waist and says, "We're not going to hurt each other, are we, doctor?" In some instances where there is a great disparity in needs, the one with the fewest needs attempts to use any compromises made as a pawn ticket to get future concessions. In the movie version of *The Godfather*, when Don Corleone agrees to help someone desperately in need in return for a future favor, what you see is an example of disparity in needs.

When there is an imbalance of needs between parties, the one with the most basic need must somehow provide himself with leverage in order to narrow the disparity. Otherwise, he is said to be in a very weak negotiating position. Countless negotiators all over the world have exercised dominance over those with more basic needs because the party in the weaker position did not utilize the leverage factors available.

Leverage Analysis

These leverage factors differ according to the negotiating situation; the amount of leverage held by either
party depends on:

1. How much you need the other party
2. How much it needs you
3. How much you need each other
4. What the other party knows that you don't know
5. What you know that is unknown to the other
   party
6. What both of you know that you don't want exposed to a third party
7. The amount of time available and how it benefits
   your position or that of the other party
8. The effect of making your problems or dispute
   known to the public, pressure groups, government
   agencies, etc.
9. The legal advantage in your favor or your opponent's
10. Peer group involvement and influence
11. Fear of failure, loss of prestige, community scorn,
    disgrace, loss of self-respect, ego, etc., on either
    side
12. The financial factor ("He who has the gold makes
    the rules")
13. The effect on future plans ("Win the battle—lose
    the war")
14. The need to be right, win praise, gain greater rec-
    ognition or press notices
15. The ability to reach organization members infor-
    mally or utilize close family ties that can influence

16. The willingness to sacrifice self for ethics, principles, or other beliefs
17. An ability to make the other party feel guilty, not loved, etc.
18. Sexual needs, preferences, hang-ups, etc.
19. A fear of the unknown or the unexpected, such as accidents, illness, death, or the hereafter
20. A deprivation of freedom of action/movement, food, clothing, etc.
21. Threat of bodily harm
22. The amount of competition available
23. Threat of boycott
24. Political influence

Now see how many additional leverage factors you can think of that were not itemized. Do this below, so that for reference purposes you will have them all together:

_____

_____

_____

_____

CREATING NEEDS

Another ingredient in the negotiating process is bringing to the surface or creating needs. The following story is an example. One day a matchmaker went to a rich merchant who had an unmarried son, and handed him a business card. The merchant said, "I'm not interested." The matchmaker responded, "You don't understand. The young lady I represent is the daughter of Baron de Rothschild." The merchant quickly replied, "Sit down. Let's talk about it." The matchmaker then went to see the baron, who did have an unmarried daughter, and also gave him a business card. The baron said, "I'm not interested," and the matchmaker responded, "But you don't understand, Baron, the young man I represent is the vice president of the World Bank." The Baron said, "Sit down, let's talk about it." The matchmaker's final visit was to the president of the World Bank, where he stated, "Have I got a vice president for you." The president quickly told him he already had too many VP's, but the marriage broker said, "The young man who is going to be your next vice president is the son-in-law of Baron de Rothschild." The president invited him to "sit down and talk about it."

We must also remember that needs come in three time frames: past, present, and future. If working on creating a need for today is not succeeding, try tomorrow's or yesterday's situation. You may be able to take advantage of a latent fear that a past problem could resurface, or you may be able to point to a possible future difficulty that can be avoided.

The Variety of Needs

Needs come in various intensities and levels of desires, as Abraham Maslow has outlined. There are those needs basic to life—air to breathe, food, and water. Then there are those that make life more enjoyable and pleasant, such as a shelter or clothing to protect us from the elements. We also have a need to be loved and cared for and to return that love. Self-respect is also an important need, for without it we are said to be full of guilt and our own worst enemy. Further, we need to be recognized and thought of as intelligent, wise, etc., although this ego need sometimes becomes master and makes puppets of us in the dance of life. Then we need to have a feeling that what we do is worthwhile, meaningful, and important. The do-it-yourself industry has certainly capitalized on this by giving us an opportunity to prove to ourselves that we can do many things ourselves instead of depending on others. We seem to have a strong need to probe, seek, search, and find out about ourselves, others, and things around us. Often, there is also a sensitive need to have things in their place, in order, and in balance.

The negotiator who recognizes how important these ego needs are and how they can influence behavior and the outcome of a negotiation, is in my opinion going to be successful in whatever situation he handles. Fail to take an opponent's ego needs into account, and you risk not being able to conclude a negotiation amicably. And even if success seems within reach, be careful you haven't failed to defer to an influential ego's needs. Someone who leaves the negotiating table feeling that his self-respect has been damaged will surely try to even the score at a later date. Someone whose ego has not been allowed to come through to demonstrate, say, a superior technical knowledge, may later torpedo your plans by making small changes whenever possible to show that your design, product, service, or argument was not perfect. Instead of working with you, he will undermine your efforts. All these needs when bundled together make a very complex mosaic. Therefore, the most difficult aspect of negotiating is anticipating and understanding the behavior of others based on their needs.

OBJECTIVES

The simplest part of the negotiating process is establishing what you want to get, what you are willing to give up and when you will do so. The difficult position comes later, when you are negotiating and attempting to achieve your goals. The difference between proving the point of your position and getting what you want should always be clear to you. Keeping this distinction in mind is very important to your success. As one outstanding negotiator once remarked, "I never lose sight of what I came to get and what I want to prove." In effect he was saying, "I subordinate my ego's needs to those needs that tend to be more fundamental." We'll discuss the defining of objectives later when we deal with preparing for a negotiating situation.

COMPROMISE

For years the word "compromise" had a very bad connotation. Now, with so many international negotiations making the news, the use of the word no longer inspires negative feelings; rather, it simply denotes making and/or getting concessions.

Most negotiations fall into three basic patterns:

Party A	Party B
1. Give, Get	Give, Get
2. Give, Get	Get, Give
3. Get, Give	Get, Give

Pattern 1: In order to be successful, the process of negotiating must include some form of compromise. What concessions are made and who makes them can differ vastly. In pattern 1 above, we see that both parties are oriented toward giving something in order to get. This type of negotiation obviously is the one with the highest probability of success. Both sides are willing to compromise, and they enter into negotiations with that thought in mind. How much and when are the details that must be worked out.

Pattern 2 also has a good possibility of success because both sides are geared toward settlement. One is open to giving, providing he subsequently gets, and the other will give as long as there is surety at the outset that something is being gotten in the exchange. The difficulty sometimes encountered in this arrangement is when one party, the getter, doesn't want to become a giver because it wants to get as much as it can before it reciprocates. In such cases, the getter presses for more and more and doesn't know when to stop. The giver then takes back concessions made, and both parties collide in their focus on getting. There are innumerable situations when parties on such a collision course have chosen not to alter their path and both wound up losing. Simple arguments with family and friends often illustrate this.

Pattern 3 is the most difficult to resolve. Unless one of the parties decides to become the giver, they both will wind up with no agreement or settlement. A role reversal must occur before any change is possible. Although the so-called hard-nosed negotiator is sometimes seen primarily as a getter, remember that there are distinct ways of becoming a getter. Note the following statements of position:

1) "Nothing you say will convince me. My mind is made up so don't bother me with facts." Until this negotiator gets, he's not giving a thing.

2) "I'm totally inflexible now, but I may change if I see or hear something worthwhile." The individual shifts from a totally uncompromising position to one of possible cooperation. Focus is still almost entirely on getting, but the possibility of compromise has at least been introduced.

3) "Whatever you show me or say had better be good." This "you're on trial" person is the easiest hard-nose to deal with because he gives you an opportunity to make your presentation. Whatever you say first and the initial impression created are extremely important.

MOMENTUM

"When you're hot, you're hot; when you're not, you're not." You have probably been in a negotiating situation where you had the sense of momentum, and you can probably also recall times when it wasn't there. "It don't mean a thing, if it ain't got that swing," as the old song reminds us. I've conducted and recorded negotiations in which momentum was present and attended others in which we would have paid dearly to have it. Some negotiations seem to hum along while others clank like the unoiled Tin Man in *The Wizard of Oz*. Taking control of the situation and causing things to happen positively is the mark of a successful negotiator. The element of momentum is commonly mentioned and written about in athletics ("Notre Dame now has the momentum and is turning this game around"); it is equally important in negotiation. (It has been my feeling for years that establishing a positive momentum early in a negotiation is one of the most important factors of success. How to get momentum going and keep it going in the right direction is discussed in greater detail later in this book.)

TIMING

Timing, as we mentioned earlier, is an aptitude many youngsters have and use when negotiating with parents. It is also part of the formal negotiating process that starts with knowing when and where to negotiate. Many an unsuccessful negotiator has later said, "If only the timing had been right." When we negotiate, what we are going to do is of course important, but *when* sometimes overshadows *what*. Serious consideration should always be given to the *when* and *where* aspects.

Unfortunately, few negotiators I have heard ever say, "Is this the right time to negotiate this?" or "Is the timing right for our demand?" or "Should we wait for another time?" or invoke some other test to determine the efficacy of the moment.

Many years ago, when I started conducting seminars on negotiating a colleague of mine said, "Hank, your timing is right." I understood what he said but didn't know if he was correct or not. That's one difficulty with timing—you don't know it's right until you try. But you can make the odds more favorable by at least considering the question of timing. If you decide the moment seems inopportune—and you have the option to postpone the issue or the negotiation—be patient.

An obvious but often overlooked point about timing: If it's not right you can't make it so. History is replete with examples of acts, ideas, and inventions that were ahead of their time. Prematurely forcing an issue does not usually strengthen your negotiating position.

ADRENALIN FACTOR

When we get excited, enthusiastic, or frightened about something, adrenalin flows through our system, pumping us up for a superior effort. That might be all right for a "fight or flight" situation where you have to run a ten-second one hundred-yard dash or scale a nine-foot wall to save your life. However, when entering negotiations mentally hyped up, you may overreact to your opponent and the action can be very damaging to your intended objectives.

Keep the butterflies in your stomach flying in formation. Stay in control of your actions. Most college football coaches know how dangerous it is to get their team too high for a game. Early mistakes due to out-of-control enthusiasm can lose games. The same applies to negotiations. You don't want later to reflect "if I hadn't been so forceful at the beginning," or "dammit, if I had only not lost my temper at his opening comments." No doubt, at some time you've experienced the butterflies taking over. Some refer to this as "choking up." For myself I've finally learned to understand this reaction by defining "choking up" merely as nerves overcoming skill.

Negotiators must overcome the adrenalin factor, first by awareness, then by action. If you are particularly keyed up, try releasing some of that pent-up energy by vigorous exercise before you negotiate. I've done this many times by going to the men's room before a session and pushing as hard as I can against a wall. Or do an isometric exercise that requires a lot of energy. I was once demonstrating how I do it to a seminar group and pushed a collapsible wall so hard I caused it to fall on the floor, and myself with it. I got up and reminded the audience that it works best on fixed walls.

BELIEF SYSTEMS

Each person brings to the negotiating table a complex belief system that is shaped and influenced by many things; such as philosophy, dogma, ethics, principles, life style, and teaching. This difference is particularly evident in labor negotiations, where management and labor often clash over belief systems. But it is not confined to one specific type of negotiating. Indeed, all negotiators, regardless of the circumstances, must be aware of conflicting belief systems and how these conflicts influence the issues.

How nice it would be if individuals could doff their belief systems like hats before going into the heat of a negotiation. Unfortunately we can't. Although a belief system is not a life-support system, it is an element that everyone relies on. It provides the frame of reference within which actions take on meanings. The skillful negotiator never loses sight of this.

Belief systems either clash or complement each other. An example in business might be a difference in the way parties view profits as a built-in factor on the price of goods. One party may take the attitude that "whatever you can get" is reasonable; another may feel that profit should "reasonably" be limited to no more than a set percentage.

When beliefs are complementary we find it hard to disagree; when they are not we find it equally hard to concur. In some instances, issues at hand are completely forgotten as the parties argue differences in beliefs. To get them to see what is happening would require a videotape of words and actions played back for awareness. Even then they might not accept the assessment.

When belief systems clash it requires an extra effort even to get agreement on what the respective differences are. What one can do is get back to discussing issues, alternatives, or any other subject that will be more rewarding. "We obviously disagree with each other based on our beliefs—let's see what we can discuss that might get us onto common ground" is a favorite expression of mine that has worked many times. A similar statement under such circumstances might get your negotiation on track again and into more promising areas of discussion.

As well as recognizing that there can be a clash of belief systems, beware of using a negotiating situation to convert another to your way of seeing things. This is not only usually beside the point; it can backfire. What is good for you is not necessarily good for another. Your needs should not dictate another's. Just because your belief system is deeply rooted and affords you peace of mind and motivates your life, it does not follow that the same results will follow if another person accepts your views.

On an international scale, transferring and exporting "isms" has achieved some very negative results: alienation of individuals, civil disturbances, breakdown of government, war. Many of today's international conflicts stem from one culture's attempting to project its ways of doing things on another culture. It rarely seems to work.

Successful negotiators likewise understand that they must *not* project their beliefs on the other party. To do so often makes the other person belligerent, defensive, hostile, or unsupportive and uncooperative. Be aware of the paramount importance of refraining from projection. Most individuals can recognize your needs and beliefs without having to be converted to them first.

3

The Negotiating Ritual

Most good negotiators have an intuitive awareness that the negotiating process is a step-by-step ritual. And, as with any ritual, there are certain consistent patterns that characterize all negotiations regardless of the goals and tactics of any specific session. These patterns should not be disturbed, and negotiators who do not realize this are usually the ones who have the most difficulty in settling differences. They tend to skip steps and then later have to return to them, which disrupts the procedure. The objective of this chapter, therefore, is to describe the flow of this ritual, showing each step along the way to the final settlement, agreement in principle, or other conclusion, whether negative or positive. Only when the ritual character of negotiating is understood can we go on to tactical details.

STEP 1: INTRODUCTORY PHASE

This step, usually brief, is designed to acquaint all the participants. Formal or informal introductions are highly recommended so that all the parties know each other's names, positions, and titles. Passing around a pad on which everyone can list this information is also a good idea. It's even more helpful if the participants' names are then typed in a list that's made available to all parties. In this way, everyone has the names correctly spelled and listed. This is useful if you are later required to write a report. It can be very embarrassing when a negotiator spends the entire day with someone and then misspells that person's name in subsequent correspondence. And addressing someone by the wrong name in the negotiating session itself is obviously no way to win points. I recall a situation when party A not only forgot the name of party B, but refused to try and find it out. He simply muttered, "Who cares? He committed the company he represents as an agent; therefore we have a deal." A few days later, B's company president called A and wanted to know how things had worked out with his agent. He was told the deal had been agreed upon, which caused the president to explode, "What idiot agreed to that?" A, having forgotten B's name, was unable to answer. The telephone exchange was reduced to a lot of name-calling and both decided it would be better not to conduct further business together. A's remembering the name would probably also have gotten a negative reaction to the deal, but not recalling the name certainly aggravated the situation.

It is helpful to use small talk during this introductory phase to get the proceedings under way in a more relaxed atmosphere. Do not, however, prolong small talk, lest the negotiation take on the feeling of a sewing circle. In some areas such as Latin America this phase often requires discussions about family or other business interests that then often extend into more lengthy sessions from which impatient North Americans sometimes have difficulty extracting themselves.

STEP 2: GENERAL OVERVIEW

The purpose of the general overview is to let the other party sense what your initial goals and feelings are without revealing much else. It is not designed for getting strong feelings off your chest. The first speaker should merely state a basic feeling, intention, or objective. Some negotiators have grave difficulties at this point because they cannot give a general overview without getting quickly into specific issues. Therefore, it is worthwhile to keep in mind the following:

1) If you are the first one to speak, keep whatever you say to a minimum and at a high level of abstraction. For example: "We are here today to negotiate this contract and hopefully reach a settlement beneficial to both parties." Such "motherhood" statements, i.e., noncontroversial statements that are difficult to contradict, are highly recommended so as not to ruffle any feathers. That comes later.

2) Allow the opposite party to respond to your opening comments before turning the negotation over to another team member. The attention span of most individuals is short—in the case of negotiations, it is very short. So let others act as a sounding board to your comments before proceeding further. Consider the process an echo test that will reveal whether your objectives and motives are different from the other party's. Now is the time to discover such differences, not later.

Plan beforehand what you think should be said in the overview, and who should say it. Like an overture to an opera, it is the last thing written but the first to be presented. It always amazes me that more negotiators don't plan this phase more thoughtfully.

3) Try not to make any irritating statements or, in general, create anger. To do so will increase overall hostility and defensiveness and diminish the possibility of cooperation and support.

Try to anticipate the response to your opening statements—role-play, in other words. If a negative reaction rather than a positive one seems likely, then change your statement.

4) Because you have such a short time—approximately one minute is appropriate to express the general overview—try to get an innocuous acknowledgment of your rough statement of situation at the outset, even if only a slight nod of the head or some other response that endorses your initial comment. If all parties are in general agreement at the outset, the road is paved for smoother negotiation.

STEP 3: "BACKGROUND MUSIC"

Most negotiators do some backtracking in order to bring the proceedings up to the present. This step is called "background music"—really the expression of stored feelings. In most negotiations, both parties usually have different ideas as to what the records indicate. Do not be surprised. In almost any situation the facts are perceived differently by the various participants. There is, for example, a strong tendency to construct the past on the basis of current beliefs. This can create a whole host of problems in your attempt to be objective about the history of whatever situation you are now included in.

I'm convinced that after the general overview both parties have to display their individual differences before progressing further. Negotiators should be prepared to accept this and recognize that allowing others to play out their background music often proves worthwhile for both parties. Impatient negotiators who short-circuit these accounts of the past with remarks such as "Well, that's history," or "Let's not emphasize the past," fail to realize that such a step is mutually beneficial. It may prevent past differences from complicating the present ones. So when the other party starts its background music, try not to interrupt. Instead, take notes on what you disagree with and then counter when you have your turn.

Finally, because the past record is so important to the settling of a negotiation, spend some time planning what you are going to say during this phase. Don't expect the words to pop out extemporaneously and flow with Churchillian eloquence. They won't.

STEP 4: DEFINITION OF ISSUES

Conflict is at the root of all issues. Early exposure of those roots is recommended during this period. Remember that most negotiators have four categories of issues: their needs, your needs, mutual needs, and finally, hidden needs. Labor and management negotiators, more than others, understand the definition of issues. They seldom attempt to negotiate any points until they draw up a laundry list of issues. These position papers, as they are sometimes called, are like road maps showing the stops that have to be made and the areas that must be passed through en route to a settlement. When defining issues, present those related to your needs, the opponent's needs, and mutual needs. Those related to hidden needs can usually be saved for later discussion.

Sometimes during this phase issues are stated and then tied to each other. That is, one issue may not be settled unless another is also resolved. Conversely, there is often an attempt to separate issues from each other, to make each mutually exclusive. Figure out whether it's to your advantage to allow issues to be tied together or not. Often it is, and allowing one issue to be completely separated from another without any maintained connection may be to your disadvantage. Remember that you're there to pursue your needs, so it helps if you tie satisfaction of the other party's needs to satisfaction of your own. Don't automatically agree to any proposal to keep issues exclusive of each other unless you've achieved your needs and are in fact prepared to settle.

There are negotiating situations in which *all* issues are explicitly bound together. No one issue is considered resolved until all have been resolved. This "packaging" of the issues is the usual practice in labor contract negotiations.

As long as you are aware of the categories that the issues fall into, you should be able to determine when tying issues together will work in your favor and when it's more to your advantage to keep them separate and distinct. Be aware that you can be flexible here, tying some issues together and treating some separately; you need not put yourself into an all-or-none situation.

Selecting the First Issue to Be Discussed

Once the issues, conditions, or problems have been out-lined and briefly discussed, you must start dealing with them one at a time. Opinions vary about whether one should introduce minor or major issues first. My feeling is that usually it is better first to discuss a minor issue that presents a strong possibility of getting an agreement in principle. The negotiating process is difficult enough without stacking the major issues at the beginning. Major issues normally do not promise easy agreement or quick settlement. Most monetary issues fall into this category, which is why they are so often relegated to the end. One exception to the minor-major pattern occurs when the parties have had a series of "on again–off again" negotiations and are sitting down together for the umpteenth time. In such instances it might be wiser to start with a major issue and relegate the minor ones for a later mop-up. This approach was taken in the 1978 Camp David meeting attended by President Carter, Prime Minister Begin, and President Sadat. At that meeting, President Carter chose to lay out the major issues for discussion first before covering any of the others. He started with the concerns about Israeli settlement in the Sinai, withdrawal from territory occupied since the 1967 war, and the West Bank problem.

"Bridge issues" are those on which individuals might meet each other halfway without any loss of ego, pride, or self-worth on either side. The agreements tend to be innocuous compromises that allow both parties to feel they got something quickly without giving too much. Bridge issues sometimes have great impact on egos and can satisfy a strong "power" motivation in the parties. The "get" aspects are usually minimal.

In a real estate negotiation, for example, a bridge issue between buyer and seller might be whether appliances—washing machine, dryer, refrigerator, etc.—are included as part of the total price for the home. If the seller originally did not consider them a part of the deal, he will now have to consider including them. This bridge issue is an excellent one to start with since neither party will want the question of appliances to undermine the potential deal. If you have, as a home buyer or seller, ever been involved in such a transaction, you probably recognize that only a very poor negotiator ever lets this blow the sale.

My wife and I once accepted a seller's price provided that the washer and dryer be thrown in with the deal. The seller refused to negotiate on this minor point, which caused us to hesitate and go into what real estate agents call "buyer's remorse." While rethinking the deal, we found another property that ultimately turned out to be far better than the first. We did not make a second offer on the first property nor accept the seller's hard-nosed position.

Bridge issues, often minor, are like flags that test the direction in which the wind is blowing and the strength of the staff that supports them. When the flag is stiff in the breeze and the staff is being moved by the wind velocity, you should recognize a danger signal—the issue raised may not be so minor. In such instances, you might consider switching over to another, less controversial, issue. Try to establish another bridge, then come back to this point later.

CONFLICT PHASE

Although you may have encountered some resistance, defensiveness, or hostility before this part of the ritual, the real volleys are now about to come your way. Eventually, as both the parties seek to gain an advantage, better their position, win or prove something, they meet head on in conflict. To be a successful negotiator, you must *not* attempt to shy away from this most important phase. For it is in the heat of such an oven that good deals are baked. The less successful negotiator often tries to avoid the heat, stress, and anxiety associated with conflict and makes premature compromises. I remember reading that "a diamond is nothing but a piece of coal that has gone through extreme heat and pressure." The jewels that sometimes come out of the tension of conflict are worth ten times the discomfort experienced. A mother might say the same thing about labor pains and the birth of her child. I'm not advocating that one create a conflict for the sake of cracking or testing others, although some might argue this point. Instead, I'm pointing out that conflict seriously tests the strength of negotiators. The way in which these tough moments are handled provides a measure of the kind of success enjoyed in business or family life in general, because conflict is part of the stuff everyday life is made of.

Although conflict—the soul of negotiation—can be a catalyst that eventually pulls both parties together, it can also be a bomb that explodes and blows both sides far apart. Handle it with care and confidence so that it serves to clarify the differences in points of view, needs, and experienced difficulties, and ventilates these through the process of negotiation.

During the conflict phase you are going to have to work to get what you "want." Be ready to be raked over the coals to prove your point. In all negotiations one party starts out by asking for what it "wants" while the opposition works to find out what the other "needs"—a confrontation that puts a great deal of stress on the process. But remember that, unlike a wrestling match, it is not a process aimed at proving one side to be the stronger. This conflict phase of negotiation is a test of strength that reveals possible areas of compromise by applying the principles of give and get.

Most successful negotiations seldom ever result in giving you what you "want"; instead, they make you struggle for what you "get." For this reason, the conflict is accentuated by a sort of polarization that seems to accentuate each party's views of what is "possible." The paradox of negotiating is clearly to be seen at this point. Each wants to get as much as he can, yet each knows a compromise is necessary, that he must in effect modify goals originally stated as absolute.

One of the difficult things encountered during the conflict phase is that both parties attempt to convince their opponents by citing examples and facts. We probably have all heard that "facts don't change anyone's mind." My experience is that an attempt to use facts and examples for this purpose usually simply evokes other, contradictory examples. If you don't believe this, the next time you're involved in a slight disagreement, just use any example to try to convince the other person to accept your view. Then listen to his "on the other hand" or "by the same token" response to prove your example is not appropriate.

Conflict in negotiating is a severe test of resolve, conviction, creativity, and ability to withstand stress. When two parties stare each other in the eye, someone has to blink. Don't be afraid either of the look or of blinking. After all, blinking lubricates the eye for better vision.

FALLBACK AND COMPROMISE

Since negotiation would be unnecessary if both parties were already in agreement, compromise is always part of the process. After the definition of issues and conflict phases comes the time to reach out for possible compromises.

The opening overtures are hypothetical statements such as "what if," "in the event of," "suppose that." Remember, however, that the fresh smell of conflict ending and compromise beginning can get many negotiators overexcited so that they underestimate their opponent. Hypothetical overtures can quickly sour if you try to nail them down too hastily. Regard them instead as trial balloons that are testing the atmosphere: Allow the balloonist to go up. You and your opponent are sounding each other out about the range of compromise possible. Remember those marvelous words uttered by Jimmy Stewart in the film *Harvey* when he outnegotiated everyone by asking, "What do you have in mind?" It is often extremely worthwhile to use the same tactic.

The question of who should make the first compromise or overture is sometimes very perplexing. I feel one should never be reluctant to make the first offer, so long as it is "give-get" oriented—which it will be if you know what you're doing and have prepared accordingly. You will compromise on something in return for getting something else. But making a first offer or concession when you are not going to receive anything is absolutely contradictory to the point of negotiating.

When offers are made that are not linked to any "get" factors, remember to echo them—that is, repeat aloud the very offer just made by your opponent. This tactic has at least three advantages: (1) The offer may be revised under the impression that your echo was a negative response and requires your opponent to submit another different offer; (2) your opponent may attempt to justify it, thus leaving himself open to further interrogation; or (3) he sells you by tempting you with further concessions that open up areas for additional compromise.

THE AGREEMENT-IN-PRINCIPLE OR SETTLEMENT PHASE

One of the most frequently asked questions at our seminars on negotiating is "How do you negotiate with someone who does not have authority?" For many years I also found that situation very perplexing and frustrating. However, I now realize that individuals with limited authority usually do not come to a settlement. But they can and do agree in principle to many things. So if you came to make a settlement and discover your opponent has not the authority to do so, change your strategy and try to nail down as many agreements in principle as possible. Otherwise your time will probably be wasted chasing settlement. In some negotiations individuals sometimes say yes as if from an ultimate authority level, then later try to bail out by changing to a no or maybe. Be aware that there is no assurance that a yes or no stated at the outset will hold throughout the negotiation.

Labor-management negotiations don't have this problem since they begin with the common understanding that the individual negotiating has the authority to speak on behalf of his group, but does *not* have authority to finalize settlement without further concurrence and ratification. But this often is a problem in other kinds of negotiation when this understanding is not always as clear as it should be.

The agreement-in-principle-settlement phase is handled more successfully when parties start recapping, summarizing where they are—what has been discussed, what agreements were reached, and even what still separates them. Yet, in videotaped negotiations that I've analyzed, I find that many individuals have difficulty in this phase primarily because they don't know that they are in it, and therefore don't recap or summarize. Indeed, it is not unusual to record a negotiation without ever hearing the words "recap" or "summary" uttered.

It also helps if both parties agree on the language to be used, because there will be less argument and dissension in the future, when terms and conditions are explicitly spelled out. I've found that writing out the details briefly on a blackboard or flip chart can help shape the language that will be acceptable later on. This also saves needing a scribe at the negotiation to take notes and be the one to give the final terms and conditions discussed and agreed to.

POST-SETTLEMENT

After the agreements and settlements have been mutually accepted comes the sometimes disruptive process of putting teeth into the agreement for monitoring subsequent compliance. Negotiations don't end when individuals shake hands on a deal or sign a piece of paper. In many cases that's when the hardest part begins. Now the agreement must be implemented and provisions made for subsequent monitoring, reporting, correcting. If an agreement is not or cannot be successfully implemented, then it can hardly be said that the negotiations were a success.

A mutual post-negotiation analysis may be the effort that saves the agreement/settlement from collapsing. Some negotiators are very hesitant to spend too much time on such matters as recourse for noncompliance or other "what if" statements that anticipate possible problems. I believe that by discussing potential snags on the crest of the high one gets from reaching a settlement, defensiveness and the likelihood of negative responses are minimized.

CHARACTERISTICS OF EFFECTIVE NEGOTIATORS

Just as the ritual of negotiation remains unchanged, so do the characteristics of effective negotiators. A client once called me and said, "Hank, I want you to tell me who the five best negotiators are so I can hire them." I told him, "I can't do that." He became very indignant and said, "All right, if you can't tell me who the best five negotiators are I want you to train the best five negotiators for me." My response was, "I can't do that either"—which was upsetting to him. He thought I could just magically turn five people into five successful negotiators. "I'll tell you what I can do for you," I said. "I can give you some of the elements that would make successful negotiators and then you can make your own selection."

Awareness

Negotiators are not born and they are not trained: They are developed over a period of time. Therefore we have to look at some of the features that make for success in negotiating.

To start with, a negotiator has to have a high degree of awareness. He has to see what's happening and be perceptive and intuitive enough to understand someone else's reaction—to sense when an individual means "I like what you are saying," "I don't like what you are saying," or "Stop; it's time to terminate." Because many negotiations are constantly on the verge of collapse, awareness is of paramount importance.

Patience

Another characteristic of a successful negotiator is patience. Impatience has a way of undermining a negotiation. The individual has to have a high tolerance for frustration and be able to cope with the extended time that negotiating takes, and with the way others behave. He must be calm when things don't work out. You can't make a good deal if you are in a hurry.

Flexibility

Another successful trait negotiators need is flexibility. They have to be able to switch from a negotiating style that is not working to other alternatives and options. Negotiators who are very rigid and inflexible will try something, and if it doesn't work they don't know what else to do. You can see how self-defeating such an attitude can be. So be careful not to develop those characteristics that make for stubborn—and unsuccessful—negotiators: the desire always to win and to be right all the time; a determination to get and never give; and an inability to say, "I don't know" or "I was wrong," these last confessions being very difficult for some people to make. But you can be persistent. The difference between a persistent negotiator and a stubborn one is that the former keeps trying different approaches, while the latter sticks to only one.

I've been asked if authoritarian personalities are inflexible and my answer is that we often see but one side of them. There are authoritarian types who can switch over to another negotiating style very quickly without missing a beat. Some inflexible individuals are less authoritarian than they are fearful of failure, whereas successful negotiators tend to be less apprehensive and more confident. This confidence enables them to vary their approach—to be dominating in one situation and very supportive in another. They can use humor and yet be deadly serious. Many successful salesmen start out by telling you a funny little story before they get serious about their products or services, all of which, of course, are supportive of your needs or designed to create new needs. Then they give you supporting data and information in a matter-of-fact manner that leads into the taking of your order. The range of styles is evident, from the personal to the informed to the businesslike. And the most successful salesman is he who can flow smoothly from one style to the next, reading you all the while for your reactions. Like salesmen, negotiators have to be very flexible in order to be successful. Being too rigid forces you into either/or situations which, as we have seen, just paint you into corners.

Attentiveness

Shakespeare wrote, "He who listens is armed," and as we will later see, poor listening is the sign of an unsuccessful negotiator. My research reveals that the average negotiator has a listener rating of 2.5 on a scale of 1 to 10—which is not too good. One barrier to being a good listener is "time sharing." Because we have the mental capacity to receive 600 words per minute and a person normally speaks at a rate of 120, our minds are often not fully engaged and we start to "share" the speaker's time with thoughts about what is going on at the office, at home, and so forth. Another reason is that we're too busy waiting for a chance to interrupt to concentrate on what the speaker is saying. And when we do interrupt, often from aggressive tendencies, we can inadvertently turn the negotiation into a confrontation. Interruptive beginnings such as "Let me tell you this," "By the same token," "On the other hand," often sound harsher than intended, because they tend to be argumentative. They will also be seen as attempts to override, intimidate, or negate what was said.

We can all become better listeners if we attempt to listen in the same time frame as the person speaking. Everyone can speak in three different time frames: about what happened yesterday (the past tense); what is going to happen tomorrow (the future tense); or what is happening today (the present tense). Learn to listen for the tense in which a person is speaking and it will force you to concentrate and thus listen better. Moreover, in negotiating conflict situations, if you can respond to your opponent in the same time frame you lessen the risk of irritating him, because he senses that you are both on the same wavelength. Not responding in the same time frame makes it appear as if you have turned a deaf ear. As an example, if you told someone you went shopping yesterday and he replied, "Well, I'm going tomorrow," that might kill your conversation. However, if he said, "You did? Did you buy anything?" he would seem interested in what you had to say.

After recording hundreds of role-playing negotiating situations on videotape, I found that individuals unknowingly turn each other off by not listening in or responding to the same time frame.

Besides the time-frame device, another exercise is to learn to listen with your head tilted to one side. It does not force you to listen, but it puts you into a listening position, and you will find yourself less likely to interrupt. Many successful salesmen have learned this as a trick to allow the buyer to speak. Negotiators should also learn this lesson and practice it.

BENCHMARKS OF A SUCCESSFUL NEGOTIATION

1) For a negotiation to be successful, both parties must first feel that the process was worthwhile, that the time consumed was productive and not just an exercise.

2) Both parties feel they got something out of the negotiation, that specific needs were satisfied. They may also sense that maybe they could have got a little bit more. As after a most enjoyable dinner, there is often a feeling of slight dissatisfaction: Even though you are satisfied with what you got, you feel you could have got a little bit more. In other words, you're still a little hungry. This applies to both parties, not just one.

3) Both parties have to leave the negotiating table with their self-respect intact, regardless of conflicts that took place, or intimidation and harassment they may have experienced.

4) Both parties also must feel that they have achieved the majority of their objectives. Since objectives differ, it is very possible for both parties to leave with this feeling.

5) No matter how skillful or experienced any individ-

ual may be, both parties should leave the negotiation with a positive feeling about having learned something from one another. I find negotiators are great students, always picking up things and constantly developing. A negotiator who feels he has failed may learn something as well, but successful negotiators inevitably apply what they learn to better effect. They learn how to conduct future negotiations more skillfully—both what to do and what not to do.

6) Both parties must feel that they wouldn't mind negotiating with each other again. Whatever took place, their attitudes should be: "It wasn't all that bad. I wouldn't mind dealing with them again." It is important to develop a good foundation for future negotiations because most negotiations are circular. You generally don't negotiate with someone just once. Frequently— particularly in business—you negotiate with him again and again.

7) Each party must leave feeling the other will comply with the agreement reached and not negate the results. Negotiations don't end with the signing of a contract, or when you shake hands. Now begins the process of living with the conditions agreed to.

CREATIVE ALTERNATIVES

Creative thinking may mean simply the realization that there's no particular virtue in doing things the way they always have been done.

—RUDOLPH FLESCH

We have already seen the advantage in considering alternatives and the benefits of planning them in advance. Too often, negotiators do not exercise their mental capabilities in generating creative alternatives. Instead, they openly discourage the search for new methods of resolving differences. Some become locked in by the dispute or conflict and refuse to test other approaches. The ability to think or say "what else?" can sometimes help us think through other possibilities. It can unplug an otherwise closed portal of investigation and conversation, whereas arbitrarily saying "I don't like it" or "It won't work," can be defeating for all concerned.

I have seen many disputes reach an impasse not because the parties' positions were so far apart, but because neither wanted to discuss alternatives. We occasionally think that we alone can come up with the most brilliant of ideas and that the other party's suggestions are impractical, foolish, or illogical. The "not invented here" or "not thought here" syndrome is a major obstacle toward reaching settlements or agreements in principle or to establishing a base for a possible compromise. Looking back on some of the least successful negotiations I've ever been involved with, I'm convinced that not listening to another person's views, ideas, and options is the principal reason for not reaching a settlement.

The negotiating process requires a mutual search for alternatives from positions that differ or separate us. Alternatives are like gears in a machine that allow it to function, move, and alter direction. Let's oil the mechanism with as many ideas as we can think of and reject none until all have been thoroughly discussed and evaluated.

To this end, I would recommend that negotiators attend a creative-thinking, synectics, or brainstorming session in which they are required to propose solutions to specific problems without rejecting any idea (alternative) while in the ideational phase. It is an exercise in self-discipline designed to get the ideas out. All ideas in a negotiation should first be recorded before discussing their merits. Only then weed out ideas that are obviously not feasible at this time or for this situation—but obvious to both parties, not just one.

Once the group has narrowed down the list, serious debate on the value of each remaining alternative can begin. And in the heated discussion of each possibility that often follows, the airing of further alternatives for possible elimination or acceptance should be accepted procedure as well. The section in this book covering major errors in negotiations has more specific methods of handling alternatives.

HIDDEN COMMUNICATION IN A NEGOTIATION

What you are speaks so loudly I can't hear what you say.
— RALPH WALDO EMERSON

Individuals communicate not only verbally but also through very clear and concise nonverbal messages. This "hidden communication," one of the most subtle aspects of the negotiating ritual, can be recognized through

1. Gestures
2. Posture
3. Facial expressions
4. Nonverbal noises
5. Silence
6. Touch

Gestures accompanied by spoken words are either congruent or incongruent with what is said. When gestures are incongruent, people tend not to believe you. As a test, try convincing your wife there is nothing wrong at work as you constantly rub the back of you neck. She'll probably spend most of the night trying to discover what is wrong. We call that the "pain in the neck" gesture.

Strong emotions are transmitted through verbal and nonverbal channels. The latter are sometimes called "feeling transmissions." Whichever term is used, the effect is the same. My own studies indicate that often when individuals cross their arms and stiffen their necks and backs, they tend not to be listening or receptive to what is being said. For a very early verification of this refer to Exodus, where the Lord called the Israelites "stiff necked," as Moses was bringing the tablets down from Mount Sinai. In addition to the crossing of the arms and the stiff back, you will also notice that non-listeners' heads tend to be held upward instead of tilted when listening. Chins go up in the air rather than down, and the fingers tensely grip the biceps or curl into a fist. Individuals who are not receptive may also rotate their bodies, as they give you a "cold shoulder," and may finally verbalize something like "Why did you say that?" or "I don't like it!"

Remember that in nonverbal communication the meaning of the message is also in the receiver, not only the sender. You may feel comfortable and positive with your arms crossed or your back and neck stiffened, but studies have shown that the reception of these gestures is negative.

The process of reading people starts the moment the negotiators walk through the door. Notice that in a group of two or more the first one who enters a room usually is the dominant one or the authority figure. He also tends to be the introducer and normally selected his seat first, either flanked by his team members or at the head of the table.

It is of additional importance to understand nonverbal communication in order to recognize when conflicts are escalating. The success of most negotiations is based on awareness of what is going on. Therefore, keeping a pulse rate of the process assists in understanding its direction and flow. As an example, individuals lean toward each other as they get ready to respond, react, make offers, get involved, or leave. Whoever once said, "he leaned towards my suggestion" or "we're getting really close together" was verbally validating a nonverbal communication. The parties were probably indeed moving physically closer together as they positively interacted to each other's needs.

Seminar attendees often want to discuss the nonverbal indications given by someone who is getting ready to call the deal off. One telling example involves individuals who wear glasses primarily to read. As long as they are receptive to what the other party is saying, the earpieces are left open while the glasses lie on the table, thus making it easier for them to put the glasses on. However, when they have decided to close their mind to others, notice how quickly the earpieces are folded—this facilitates putting them away in a case or in a pocket and indicates their imminent departure.

Cigarette smokers also have some revealing gestures. They tend to put out each cigarette at approximately the same length, with the same kind of rotation. When faced with a situation in which they would like to leave or terminate the session, the smoker often extinguishes his cigarette when it is longer than the others smoked. Observing the longer cigarette butt in an ashtray filled with ten others will give you a clue as to what the other party may be planning—as will all these subtle and minute gestures.

Another source of nonverbal information is called the toe-up message. It has been recorded in many video-taped sessions that when parties are very tense, irritated, uptight or worried, they tend to stiffen up the lower leg muscles in the calf and cause the toes to point upwards. More relaxed individuals or group members tend to have toes that are not raised.

As an experiment, cross your legs and tense your leg muscles, making the toes rise. Hold that position for a while. Note that the muscle sometimes cramps after holding that position too long, and you'll understand how the initial tension can create a reinforcing discomfort.

Silence in a negotiation is as significant as gestures. We now realize that most silence periods exceeding five seconds are meaningful, although the meaning may vary. For example, sometimes silence means, "Give me time to think"; sometimes, "I'm getting ready to tell you something." Notice how often disclosure is usually preceded by a silence as the individual thinks, "Should I tell them," or "Is this the time to. . . ." Silence can also mean "I'm ready to make a deal, make me an offer" or "It's time to leave." It may not always be possible to figure out exactly what a silence means in a given instance, but if you are aware that it has significance, you will be prepared.

Many seminar attendees ask "Can I get away with faking nonverbal communication?" Contriving gestures and postures may be possible for a short time, but seldom will someone get away with it for long. Like telling lies, one pretense is much easier to hide than two or three. The reason is that you cannot control your subconscious gestures, which will eventually emerge as incongruent with your conscious action. The result is that the receiver tends not to believe you. We all seem to possess a fail-safe mechanism that registers as nonverbal messages are received. It automatically encodes all of them and, if incongruent, the readout says "tilt." Something is wrong. This may be part of our survival kit for sensing danger in what behavioral scientists call the "fight or flight" situation.

One short-term gesture that does seem to work is the one associated with confidence. The fingertips are joined together to form a pyramid—what has been called "steepling." Remember the movie *The Inspector General* with Danny Kaye? He merely lay back and mumbled as he steepled, causing those he was interrogating to think he knew where all the skeletons were hidden. You might use this gesture in a situation in which you want nonverbally to communicate "I'm stronger than you think" or some similar message. It can also mean "I'm thinking very seriously about what you just said."

In summary, it is very important to be aware of nonverbal communication because through it people tell you how they feel or think. Understanding how a person is reacting to what is taking place is vital to success in negotiations. It enables you to exercise with a clearer sense of direction whatever option, alternative, strategy, or tactics you want to implement. Moreover, as you take action, nonverbal feedback tells you whether you should continue or if a change is required. You can avoid unhappy endings if, monitoring nonverbal clues, you read clearly the message that it is time to close the deal or end the session. Overkill—talking oneself out of a deal—is a common occurrence that can be minimized by paying attention to the signals given off by others, whether or not they are actually speaking.

4

The 1962 Cuban Missile Crisis: A Case Study in Negotiation

Let's look at some of the principles of negotiating discussed in the first three chapters, in a historical case study. The conflict between the United States and Russia in 1962 concerning deployment of Russian offensive missiles in Cuba provides an excellent situation for analysis, particularly because it involves double negotiations: first, among the Americans, as various members of the government discussed how best to handle the situation; and second, between the Americans and the Russians. The entire world held its breath awaiting the outcome, for if the dispute were not successfully negotiated, World War III might follow.

One of the finest TV documentaries I've ever seen was "The Missiles of October," produced by the American Broadcasting Company. It dealt with the discovery of Soviet missiles in Cuba, the subsequent planning of what to do, and the confrontation and negotiations that followed.

The situation became history when it was discovered by aerial U-2 photographs that the Soviet Union had placed missiles in Cuba. This was shocking, since an intelligence agency had advised the president that "the Soviet Union would not make Cuba a strategic base." It pointed out that the Soviet Union had "not taken this kind of step with any of its satellites in the past."[1]

After having seen the film many times while using it as a case study in a negotiating laboratory, and having read Robert Kennedy's account of the incident in his *Thirteen Days,* I came to the following conclusions.

History is not an accurate sage. *One of the major problems many negotiators have is that they make track-record assumptions,* that is, that if something has previously occurred, it probably will recur in the same way. Or, as in the missile case, because it had not happened, it wouldn't. At best history prepares us for things to look out for and warns us not to accept readily previous happenings or behavior. *Some negotiations are very unpredictable and success is achieved only if we are not put off or lulled by the track record.*

In September 1962, a month before the U-2 photos were taken, agents in Cuba had reported Soviet missile installations and one commented that a drunken Cuban pilot had boasted about them. But instead of being immediately passed on to the president, this information was checked further. As Robert F. Kennedy stated of

1. Robert F. Kennedy, *Thirteen Days.* (New York: W. W. Norton, 1969), p. 20.

the delay, "in retrospect, this was perhaps a mistake."[2] *Any information, whether confirmed or unauthenticated, should always be passed on to the person ultimately responsible.* Many a negotiator can recall an incident of not being advised of something by someone because that person didn't think it important enough. Such a judgment can be very costly and dangerous. *The person who signs the checks needs to know what for.*

The president's advisory staff immediately agreed that action was to be taken as a result of the U-2 photos. What that action would be was the purpose of the meetings. *In preparing to negotiate it is usually advisable to reach an early agreement in principle.* I've been to and observed sessions where the members not only didn't agree in principle but undermined any attempt to get accord on the direction in which they might go. *And you can't get to where you're going if you don't know where you are.*

When preparing for a very serious and important negotiation it is sometimes worthwhile to gather the decision maker's staff and let them argue and fight with each other about which path to follow. And *after* they have done so, allow the person who signs the checks to decide the course of action. When President Kennedy's cabinet and advisers did this, it resulted in a united commitment that paved the way for dealing successfully with the Soviet Union. It is also better before going into a fight to know whom you can depend on.

Initially most of the discussion on what course of

2. Ibid., p. 29.

action to follow concerned military strikes. When another alternative, a blockade, was introduced, the majority quickly rejected it, arguing their case strongly. It was suggested, for example, that the Soviets might be provoked into setting up a blockade of Berlin in retaliation. There is an automatic reject button that eliminates other ideas, concepts, alternatives, options, and it is a real problem in many negotiations. But, as the outcome of the missile crisis proves, *every possible course of action should be seriously discussed, no matter how implausible or ineffective it first appears.* And in evaluating options, *our best friends are named who, what, where, when, why, and how.*

The Americans knew that the Russian missiles would be operational within seven days and therefore that action would have to be taken before the week was out. No matter how much time we think we *need* to prepare adequately for a negotiation, there is always the amount of time we *have.* So we make it happen and condense the span-time to meet the deadline. *There is never enough time to do the job right, but enough time to do it.*

When the president questioned what Soviet reaction might be to a military attack, he was told that there would be no counterattack. We should all be thankful that he did not accept this advice. Years later in Vietnam, we were to learn that our bombing missions against Hanoi served only to increase North Vietnamese resistance and dedication. Almost always, *the tougher the tactics, the tougher the resistance.*

At the end of the first day of talks the two options

under discussion were a military strike and/or a block-ade. These two later generated further alternatives: getting favorable support from other countries and obtaining United Nations approval for subsequent action. *It is important to develop fallback positions early on so as to be flexible and not rooted in one direction.* The discussion can then follow through on why you should compromise, and what you get in return if you do. *Contingency plans serve to increase your range of future options.*

After the proponents of a military strike concluded their argument, they explained that "our struggle against Communism throughout the world was far more than physical survival—it had as its essence our heritage and our ideals." Robert Kennedy goes on to say that "we spent more time on this moral question during the first five days than any other single matter."[3] *Morals, ethics, and principles therefore, do influence negotiators' actions*—as we saw earlier in our discussion of belief systems.

Before the missiles were sighted the president had scheduled an appointment with the Soviet ambassador. He now decided to use it as a testing ground. He said nothing about what he had learned, but rather listened as he was told that USSR interest in Cuba was purely agricultural and that the only weapons supplied were defensive. The president then read from his previous statement that touched on the use of Soviet offensive weapons in Cuba. Thus he allowed the ambassador an opportunity to reveal or lie. The lie that followed re-

3. Ibid., p. 39.

affirmed to the president that the Russians' nefarious action was going to continue, while the recap itself made the ambassador wonder whether the president knew something that he didn't disclose.

Two lessons can be learned from the president's tactics: first, that *recapping serves to prevent misunderstandings, as well as make an opponent uneasy if he has something to hide; second, that the successful negotiator has to know when and how much to disclose.* As Frank McKinney Hubbard said, "A diplomat is a fellow that lets you do all the talking while he gets what he wants."

The arguments between those who favored military action and those who supported a blockade continued heatedly for two and a half days. Finally, a majority agreed to the blockade, but only after long hours and fatigue took their toll. *Some people under stress in negotiations change their positions; others dig in deeper.*

Robert Kennedy described the discussion among the president's staff: "For every position to be taken there were inherent weaknesses."[4] *There are no single solutions to complex problems*—despite those political hopefuls who offer simplistic answers to our myriad difficulties. Although we seek out the *best* alternative, we recognize that it is not the *only* one. I strongly suggest that *if* you ever reach a point where you think you have *the* answer, step aside and ask yourself, "What else?" You may find that you have isolated the solution to one possibility because you either could not come up with more alternatives or were not prepared to

4. Ibid., p. 44.

deal with them. *No matter what answer you come up with, there will always be others; some possibly better, some certainly worse.*

After advising our allies around the world about the quarantine action, the president informed the American people on national television of his decisions; he also advised the Soviet ambassador through the secretary of state—one hour before his TV address. The ambassador left the meeting visibly shaken[5] —the Russians now knew we knew. *Use strategic demands or the disclosure of information to set the stage for your negotiations.*

In his speech to the nation, the president emphasized that the blockade action would be an initial step, but he didn't elaborate on what he would do if the quarantine failed to work. His objective was to wait for the Russians' response before going any further. *Turn over cards one at a time. Tactics work best if you try them and then wait to see what happens.* Don't undermine your objectives by playing so many cards that you lose sight of your goal.

One of the most unusual aspects of the entire incident was that the Soviets neglected to conceal the missiles on the ground. Not until one week after they were spotted by our U-2 aircraft was camouflage started. Robert F. Kennedy wrote, "it was never clear why they waited until that late date to do so."[6] My belief is that the missiles were not concealed because the Russians *wanted* us to photograph them and then waited to see

5. Ibid., p. 53.
6. Ibid., p. 58.

what would happen. Probe and see. They even went further by lining up their aircraft on the ground, wing tip to wing tip, thus making them an inviting target. Obviously, they believed that cooler heads would prevail and no air strike would be called. *Like good negotiators, they probed, tested, and checked out the other party's position and possible reaction.*

The president advised Premier Khrushchev of the blockade and requested his observance of the guidelines imposed. In so doing, he also spelled out what would happen if the blockade were breached. The threat of a mutually destructive confrontation was in the air. *When things seem about to collapse around you, it sometimes helps to tell the other party it may go down with you,* that a rash act or decision might trigger disaster for both of you. *Egos can sometimes be kept in control by subordinating them to larger issues.* Successful negotiating is not a contest to see who can hold his breath the longest. It is a process that enables all to breathe easier.

Neither side wanted nor was prepared to go to war over the incident. Therefore, both were careful not to put the other into a "chicken" position that would cause an emotional response, prompting the parties to overreact. The president sent his brother Robert to visit the Russian ambassador and make this point clear. *Don't paint yourself or others into a corner. Allow enough room to maneuver a way out.* Make your point without making an enemy.

Once the blockade was enforced the first test came when two Russian ships approached the quarantine barrier. Then a Russian submarine surfaced between them. The three ships continued slowly, like a stiff-legged western marshal walking towards the challenge of a gun duel. Then the Russian ships stopped and turned around. The confrontation was avoided. The guns never came out of the holster. *When you have taken a position in a negotiation, be prepared for the test that usually comes.*

During the height of the conflict, the international wires hummed with messages. From the moment President Kennedy announced his action, he opened up lines of communication with Khrushchev. Although some of the messages were taken by the Russian as subtle or implied threats, he continued to communicate. *Keeping open lines of communication minimizes the chances of a final breakdown in negotiations. Letting off hot air is less dangerous than throwing punches.*

Khrushchev offered not to send additional weapons to Cuba, and to withdraw or destroy those already there. In return, he wanted the United States to stop the blockade and promise not to invade Cuba. Kennedy and his staff made a grave mistake here. *They should have responded that the offer was received and was being evaluated, indicating, "We'll think it over and get back to you."* That type of response doesn't say yes or no, while at the same time it indicates consideration. Instead, no response was made while the Russian proposal was being carefully examined. A second proposal from Khrushchev followed twelve hours later—the first one was still unanswered. The second offer was considerably more demanding, including the removal of U.S. Jupiter missiles from Turkey in return for a Soviet guarantee not to interfere in Turkish political affairs. *When a proposal is made, tell the other party you have received it and are considering it. Silence in these circumstances can make your opponent feel he is being ignored—to which he may respond with greater demands.* When you receive an offer, first tell the other party you received it—then act.

After much confusion about the change in tone from the first to the second proposal and how to answer the latest offer, Robert F. Kennedy suggested responding to the first proposal *only*. What followed was a brilliantly worded recap of what the initial proposal consisted of and who would do what to whom. From that point on, the confrontation settled into a negotiation and the rest became history. Two great nations faced each other, tested the other's commitment and determination, and finally *negotiated* their differences.

In summary, the outcome was a win-win negotiation because Khrushchev's objective was to secure "Castro's Cuba from the standing threat of invasion,"[7] and ours was to remove the missiles from Cuba without military intervention. Khrushchev further stated that "when we put our ballistic missiles in Cuba, we had no desire to start a war. On the contrary, our principle aim was only to deter America from starting a war which, started over Cuba, would quickly expand into a world war."[8]

7. Edward Cranshaw, *Khrushchev Remembers.* (Boston: Little, Brown, 1970), p. 488.
8. Ibid., p. 495.

5

Mistakes Committed
by Negotiators

Winning the negotiation depends not only on doing the
right thing but also on avoiding the wrong thing. Following the order of the ritual consciously, without an
awareness of habits or attitudes that work against success, is a true exercise in wasting time. I therefore
particularly urge your attention to faults commonly
revealed by poor negotiators.

POOR LISTENING

As previously stated, most negotiators are not very good
listeners. At an early age we are instructed on how to
speak, write, and read, yet the skill of listening is con-
spicuously absent from school curricula around the
world. When one considers how much listening is re-

quired, it becomes evident how extremely important it is to improve that skill.

Negotiators must become *excellent* listeners in order to "hear" what is going on in another person's mind, for what is verbalized often is only part of the entire message. Careful listening will reveal, for example, when someone is not responding in the same time frame. This will give you an important perception about that person's unspoken feelings. It is sad to realize how many arguments were started not by conflict, but by poor listening. Negotiators were given two ears and one mouth—that has a message for us. I recommend you try the exercises for better listening outlined in this book.

POOR USE OF QUESTIONS

After so many years, I'm still amazed at how few questions are asked during a negotiation. Typically, four to six individuals over a period of one hour will ask about eight to ten questions—very few, considering that questions do a variety of practical things: direct, control, inform, intimidate, reveal, and lead. This discovery becomes more evident when sessions are recorded on videotape so that participants see and hear the limited number of questions used.

When the problem is discussed in our seminar, the following are cited as the principal reasons why few questions are asked:

1. Desire to control—questions turn the discussion over to the other party

2. Reluctance to appear ignorant
3. Fear of the answers
4. Questions inspire anxiety and defensiveness, feelings that are often difficult to deal with in others

However, I believe questions are relegated to a secondary position because when we negotiate we are attempting to change, convince, sell, persuade, or influence others. Therefore, we make statements and support them with data, information, or examples. In this framework, questions do not seem applicable, so they are not frequently employed. What is happening actually is a focus to such an extent on fixed opinions that an exploration of alternatives is seriously impeded.

Many negotiators discuss with others what questions they should or will ask. Unfortunately, they often completely forget to ask them. It isn't until they leave the negotiation that they remember the questions. But it's too late. The timing is way off.

Questions are to a negotiator what a pipe wrench is to a plumber: a necessary tool, to be used at the right time to keep things flowing smoothly. Accepting the "reasons" not to ask questions betrays a lack of confidence that the process or ritual is an effective one. And like a self-fulfilling prophecy, negotiations in which questions are few are frequently exercises in futility.

Another interesting aspect of questions is that many are answered by the person asking them instead of the listener. Some negotiators who ask a question cannot stand more than five seconds of silence. (Interviewers are especially guilty of this.) Anything beyond this seems to cause anxiety and prompts them to answer their own questions as shown here.

Question	Own answer
"Where did you get these material costs from?"	"Did you get them from ____"
"Why do you feel this way?"	"Is it because ____"

We have already seen that silence itself can be an indication of many things, both positive and negative. If we do not patiently wait to see which response it is, we may talk too much and thereby weaken our position. On a major U.S. defense contract, the contracting officers were specifically instructed not to answer any question asked by the notoriously impatient contractor in less than five seconds. The tactic worked like a charm, for the contractor talked himself out of a large sum of money.

Seminar attendees state that they usually do not spend much time preparing questions. Only a few take the trouble to write them out as a part of their preparation. But lack of discipline in preparing questions may explain why we think about possible problems too late. Unfortunately recall usually comes afterward— while driving back to the office or going down in the elevator.

Asking questions is a skill that must be developed. Some persons have mastered it by recognizing that questions often cause anxiety. Therefore, to minimize the other's anxiety they give information to get some in return—"I've got a tough boss to convince, so before I approach him with your proposal you had better give me a lot of information."

Some persons will ask too many questions that can be answered by "yes" or "no"—which just puts the ball back in their own court. If you have questions that aim at eliciting information in some detail, try to phrase them so as to get the other person to provide a response you can evaluate. Rather than, "Do you have any other ideas?" say "What else can we do?"

Questions are a negotiator's guide to directing, controlling, informing, and revealing. But they are often poorly used. More time spent in preparing which questions to ask and how to ask them will reward you with the dividend of more successful negotiations.

BADLY HANDLED DISCLOSURE OF INFORMATION

In many negotiations individuals have occasion to disclose something to the other party. As we have seen in the analysis of the Cuban missile crisis, *when* and *how* information is disclosed is vital to the success of the negotiation. The more effective negotiator has learned to disclose incrementally, while the less successful one engages in "gut-spilling."

Incremental disclosure consists of revealing information a little at a time; gut-spilling means telling everything without any interaction or pauses. Incremental disclosure tends to be more credible than gut-spilling because it involves more interaction with the person opposite you. That person feels more opportunity to control the direction of the information-gathering process and so is more confident of the information's reliability.

Disclosure is a bilateral process rather than a unilateral one. You might say there is the discloser and the disclosee. The latter starts pumping for information and the former is expected to supply some. The flow should be controlled by the one who is priming the pump. This is the person who has the strong need for getting something out of the faucet. While small squirts of information are preferable to none, the disclosee is likely to become very suspicious when a small effort to get disclosure is followed by a gush of data.

Do I mean that gut-spilling has no part in our society? It does—on the analyst's couch. In therapy the analyst expects the patient to "gut-spill"; if he instead receives incremental disclosure, it makes the work more difficult. But the analyst's couch is not the negotiating table, and a different form of disclosure is recommended.

Sometimes imminent disclosure can be anticipated by pauses in conversation. Many times individuals pause for five seconds as they consider whether to reveal something, almost as if they were having a last-minute thought about how much to disclose. On such occasions, test by saying "What else?" or "What more should I know?" or some other such question.

MISMANAGING PRESENTATION OF ISSUES

Many a negotiator successfully manages the initial phases of the negotiating ritual, developing a noticeable sense of confidence that is all too quickly shattered once the parties begin addressing themselves to the specific issues. In this situation the difficulty usually lies in a failure to realize that there are different phases in the discussion of issues, and that confusion on this point inevitably hinders movement toward achievement of goals in the negotiating session. It is also true that some issues can be resolved without passing through more than the single discussion phase, and that, of course, compounds the likelihood of confusion for the unaware, who may expect *all* issues to be amenable to settlement through immediate discussion.

It is evident enough to all that no issue can be resolved without a discussion of the issue itself. However, what is not always so evident is that often this discussion should be deferred pending a gathering of pertinent information that may not yet be at hand. Be sure to avoid the mistake of moving into a discussion of a substantive issue before all the relevant data is in hand. Trying to resolve an issue before completion of a necessary fact-finding phase is worse than spinning your wheels and getting nowhere. More likely than not it will lose you ground. Make sure that from your side all questions surrounding the issue have been researched.

Similarly, be attentive to the possibility of prospective problems arising in conjunction with a proposed settlement of an issue. What frequently helps here is working for an agreement in principle, because problems can generally not be ironed out until something actually does go wrong. An agreement in principle promotes amicable handling of the potential difficulty. An attempt to solve a specific problem before it occurs, on the other hand, is likely only to get you bogged down in differences on how it will surface, why it will surface, and what exactly to do about it, none of which gets you past a negative type of speculation that may well prove unnecessary. Recognize possible problem areas; work for agreement in principle in those areas. Avoid getting into tying an agreement to the solution of a problem that might arise. You'll find yourself getting sidetracked from the point at issue and focusing on incidental or theoretical differences that can complicate your situation.

Before going into a negotiation, work to divide your issues into categories according to the phases they will need to pass through. You will probably find that certain issues can go right into discussion on the substance of differences and similarities in outlook. But others, you will find, require further research to assure that you have all the facts you need at your disposal in order to pursue your objectives effectively. And in yet other instances you'll realize that potential problems may arise, but you can work for agreements in principle in those areas that may prove problematic. Organize your issues according to categories of "ready for discussion, " "need more information," and "may raise a further problem," and you'll find yourself managing their presentation to much better effect.

CONFUSING NEGOTIATION WITH DEBATE

Earlier on, we saw the difference between confronting an opponent and negotiating with him, between taking an either/or instead of an if/then position. Failure to recognize the distinction can be problematic; delivering ultimatums is antithetical to the negotiating process. However, more negotiators have a problem with maintaining a distinction in another area: They frequently confuse negotiating with debating. And in a determination to win points in argument, they lose the process.

Here are some points to clarify the differences between negotiating and debating:

Negotiating	Debating
1. Win/win	1. Win/lose
2. Cooperative	2. Adversary
3. Flexible	3. Inflexible position
4. Often no third party	4. Influence third party
5. Make concession	5. Make no concession
6. Ask questions	6. Don't ask questions—make statements
7. Usually interested in other party's needs	7. Not interested in other party's needs

Both debaters and negotiators have the same objective: winning. *How* they seek to win rather than lose is the difference. The important point is to recognize this difference, so that you can negotiate when you want to, but debate when it is in your best interest. At times you will want to prevail in the discussion on differences of fact or opinion. But know what you're doing.

Unfortunately, in most of the negotiating sessions we have evaluated in our seminars, the participants did *not* know which they were doing until we played back the video tape and they could clearly see and hear the distinction. Debating and negotiating are inexorably tied together. I've yet to observe, record, or attend a negotiation in which individuals were not doing both.

However, for the purposes of achieving objectives, negotiators have to perceive clearly the dissimilarities. Debaters do *not* attempt to reach settlements or agreements, whereas negotiators, to be successful, *must* reach them. In some instances, debating produces a negative effect on negotiating by making the opponent stiffen his resistance and even become defensive. Yet the two are like an on-off switch that controls the lights of a room. Sometimes you want it dark and at other times you want it light. The choice is yours to exercise.

OVERREACTING TO STRESS

Harry Truman's comment about staying out of the kitchen if you can't stand the heat applies to almost everyone who negotiates any situation in which there are strong differences and a clash of needs. If you cannot withstand these factors, they will start to rule your emotions and hence, your actions. Because a dispute or conflict will probably bring out stress, anxiety, threats, insults, or sarcasm, prepare yourself beforehand to deal with them. How? Let's take threats as an example.

When asked what they would do if threatened in a

negotiation, the typical responses of seminar attendees are:

1. Counter (threaten back)
2. Walk out
3. Ignore
4. Change the subject
5. Use levity (joke or laugh at it)

Many threats arise in negotation because individuals get emotional and sometimes say things they later wish they hadn't said. (And sometimes persons at a further point say what they wish they had said sooner to "get things off their chest.")

To handle a threat, try the following. When a threat is perceived or received, whether expressed or implied, clarify it—not by saying, "You're threatening me, aren't you?" but by saying, "I took that as a threat. I don't know if you meant it that way." The other party will either emphatically state, "That's right!"—or, "It wasn't meant to be a threat" and subsequently soften the words and position.

Be prepared to react to the first possibility. Threats, after all, are verbal expressions of emotional needs and sometimes best kept in view. At other times they are better passed over, because it's not the best time to deal with them. In either case, by clarifying whether or not a threat was intended, we give the other person a chance to exercise control over his emotions.

The nature of negotiations seems to cause conditions of stress that effect and influence all of us. Yet, if that nature is understood and dealt with, we can control it rather than having it control us.

REJECTING ALTERNATIVES

All of the advice given earlier about considering and creating alternatives will be of no help if, in a real negotiating situation, you prematurely reject them.

It is amazing how often people reject alternatives without taking the time to evaluate their worth. Quick statements such as "Is that all you have to offer?" or "That will never work," are perceived as automatic rejection.

Minimizing the importance of another person's alternatives may work against your needs. Remember that the original shape or package in which an alternative is presented can be altered to suit you if you simply massage it by asking how, where, when, why, what, and who. Those outstanding six friends assist us in understanding and learning more about specific alternatives or options.

The creative negotiator constantly seeks alternatives and doesn't make a quick judgment as to whether an option is good or bad. You can probably recall negative reaction to some concept that, after further deliberation and thought, you accepted, perhaps in an altered form. Alternatives and options are not submitted for an early death, but for a question-and-answer assessment of whether they are acceptable for further discussion. In this regard, one interesting aspect of massaging alternatives is that by asking for more information, the person who winds up rejecting the idea is sometimes the one who originally presented it.

NOT DISCLOSING HOW YOU FEEL

Although none of us can completely conceal our negative feelings (we usually reveal them nonverbally), few ever disclose them with remarks such as "I'm disgusted," or "I feel frustrated." There are times when this reticence to express feelings is best put aside. I learned this lesson well years ago in a negotiation. My opposite party and I were getting nowhere in the discussions and both of us felt frustrated. My opponent stood up and pulled out of his briefcase a small windup toy—a man who walked around in circles. He wound him up, and as the toy man circled my desk, my opponent said, "I feel like this poor bastard!" His action made me laugh and I said, "I do too!" He then responded, "If you feel that way, and so do I, let's do something about it." We did. That simple act brought home a clear message: It's sometimes a good idea to let others know how you feel. Just make sure you don't at the same time accuse the other of causing a feeling of frustration or annoyance— that usually leads to an angrier situation. Keep the "I" messages clear and lower the "you" ones. Don't point fingers at others; point them at yourself.

MISUSE OF TEAM MEMBERS

If you take one or more people with you to a negotiation, you will have more eyes, ears, and minds. But only if every member of the team is given a specific assignment will his participation be productive. Often when a negotiating team goes into a session, its members are not properly used. Their possible contribution is minimized by asking for someone to furnish information at inappropriate times or without any lead-in. And a division of responsibilities, which is frequently very useful, is never made. Although there is always a need for someone to concentrate on picking up nonverbal cues, for example, many teams do not assign any member to this task. Some team leaders or spokesmen are fearful that members will speak out of turn or say something they shouldn't. But this need not be of concern if the leader carefully prepares his team for the part each member is to play—somewhat like a quarterback calling signals and handing the ball off to another player.

PROBLEMS IN INTRA-ORGANIZATION NEGOTIATING

One of the largest U.S. corporations once asked me to conduct a negotiation seminar for their personnel, emphasizing the reasons why individuals tend to negotiate better with other organizations than they do with their own. At the root of this request was the awareness that we usually resolve conflict better with strangers than we

do with those we know well. Think of the times you've
been able to deal with a dispute with your neighbor, but
were unable adequately to handle one within your own
family.

After many years of conducting seminars, I've found
at least six reasons why this phenomenon occurs.

First, when we negotiate with another organization's
representative, we are engaged in needs that look something like this:

Company A	Company B
Principal's needs	Principal's needs
Agent's needs	Agent's needs

When two agents negotiate for two separate principals,
each knows and acknowledges the specific needs the
other brings to the meeting. One agent does not question
that the other agent *knows* what is good for his principal. However, when individuals negotiate within a
company, the outline of needs looks like this:

	Principal	
Agent A		Agent B

They both have a common principal—the company—
and each believes he knows exactly what is good for the
company. They clash not only because they have individual differences, as was the case with the president's
staff during the Cuban missile crisis, but because they
disagree on what is best for their organization. In intra-
organizational disputes, extremely sensitive feelings

exist about who is doing the best job for the company. And sometimes the argument centers on who is undermining the common objectives by their actions. This sort of finger-pointing exercise seldom occurs in inter-organizational conflicts.

When we negotiate externally we try to understand what the other party's needs are so as to ensure the success of the negotiation. We enter many intra-organizational situations, however, with the ego-oriented emphasis on what *we* want, often without ever giving consideration to the other party's wants or needs. We say things like "This is what I want,"or "When are you going to start supporting our efforts?" But because both party's needs are paramount in a negotiation, you can't toss aside your opponents regardless of how you perceive them. They must be thought about, discussed, argued, and considered for compromise. Our own needs are only one half of the puzzle—the other pieces must fall into place for the entire picture to be complete.

It is amazing how many individuals approach internal matters through confrontation instead of negotiation; they use a ramrod principle that they know would not work outside the organization, where velvet gloves are in order.

I recall a manager for whom I worked many years ago. He was known by his subordinates as "old iron-ass," due to his Prussian methods of driving, directing, and intimidating employees. Yet if you were ever with him when a very important contract had to be negotiated, he was an "old smoothie" in the way he handled outsiders. The manager clearly understood that his approach to members within the organization wouldn't work outside the organization. Despite his attitude toward employees and co-workers he realized the point that the stronger the tactics, the greater the resistance. After you've confronted an opponent, even if your needs were satisfied, he will wait for a chance to settle the score. Hitler's troop commanders certainly learned this lesson when they terrorized and humiliated millions in their occupation and, as a result, increased partisan resistance. Mistreatment is sometimes forgiven but seldom forgotten.

We tend to behave more as devil's advocates with our own people than with outsiders because we think it will benefit all concerned. We sometimes think appearing more cynical and skeptical, frowning more and smiling less will make for a better meeting. No doubt you can identify with this circumstance when you recall how easy it can be to sell a client and how hard to convince the boss. Somehow the boss can come up with more arguments against a proposal than the client ever will.

There tends to be less of a power struggle when we negotiate externally. For whatever reasons, our ego needs seem to be stronger when dealing with superiors, peers, or subordinates than they are with outsiders. One possibility is that we are more "get"-oriented externally. Internally we often attempt to *prove* things to others.

When egos clash with issues, egos usually prevail. Successful negotiators know this and try not to let that confrontation happen.

Individuals tend to be more sensitive and thin-skinned

in an intra-organizational situation. Comments made by an outsider that may be totally ignored raise anger when uttered by a co-worker. Personalities clash and problems and issues are put in a secondary position. Maybe the saying "only those that know and love you can hurt you" applies.

Overwhelming evidence proves that we are far more win-win oriented in inter-organizational disputes than in intra-organizational ones, where the win-lose approach is used. Individuals appear to give or compromise more easily when dealing with outsiders than with those inside the organization. We sometimes are more generous with total strangers than we are with our colleagues or friends.

Conversely, we also tend to be more successful with outsiders because we realize that if we *don't* negotiate we both lose! This lose-lose prospect seems to influence our actions and as a result, in negotiating we make concessions, change positions, or say, "We were wrong." Within our organization, the tendency is to believe that the other person's loss inevitably results in our own gain. This is a clear fallacy when you take into account the negative effect that ego competition can have on the organization's operations.

6

Alternatives at an Impasse

All negotiators can nominate at least one negotiation that would qualify as the world's toughest. But they would probably withdraw their candidate when apprised of the following situation.

THE CASE OF THE U.S. EMBASSY IN MOSCOW

In 1962 the Russians and Americans sat down to discuss the construction of a new U.S. embassy building in Moscow. As of early 1979, however, the only measure of progress was a large hole on ten and one-half acres of land. Even the pyramids in ancient Egypt met better schedules than that. The problems that have held up construction are many; more than once the parties have reached an impasse.

Although the two parties have been negotiating to build the embassy in Moscow, the terms are influenced by the construction of a new Soviet embassy building in Washington. So in a typical political tactic, both sides have agreed that each must start work at the same time and neither is to move in until both buildings are completed. Because American construction companies are more reliable, it was feared that the Soviet embassy in Washington might be finished well in advance of the U.S. Embassy in Moscow. The clauses to prevent this have taken considerable time to work out. Construction of the Soviet Embassy was contracted to an individual builder. In Moscow, where construction is government operated, the project manager found himself dealing with various government bureaus and, consequently, a mass of red tape. He found out that no one had authority to make a decision about anything—a case of Boris saying, "I have to report to Igor," and Igor saying, "I have to report to Ivan"—the old "limited agent" routine.

Specification and selection of materials has become a nightmare—whether to use American ceramic tile, or Russian plumbing fixtures, or U.S.-made bricks, etc. Finally, a decision was made to ship everything except steel and concrete from the West. Just consider the logistical problems involved in such an arrangement. It is estimated that, as a result, the project will take at least one more year to build in Russia than it would have in the United States. Also, because of the newness of the imported materials, the Russian workers must be trained in working with everything from conduit pipes to copper tubing and other materials not normally used in the Soviet building industry.

Another major problem is security checks to ensure that no Soviet "bugs" are planted, especially during the early stages of construction. Daily U.S. security checks will be used to make sure that the building is clean of such listening devices.

It has taken two years just to translate into Russian the blueprints, which weigh more than three hundred pounds.

Finally, even if work is started soon, it undoubtedly will be delayed by the 1980 Olympics in Moscow, which have a priority over any other industrial or commercial building projects.

As one writer stated, "the subject, while simple in conception, makes other U.S.–Soviet negotiations look like rubber stamp debates."

BREAKING DEADLOCKS

Despite the seemingly unsurmountable difficulties, the Americans and Russians did manage to arrive at an agreement on the project. This should illustrate that when an impasse or deadlock has been reached, there are still likely to be alternatives available. The successful negotiator recognizes the many possibilities and explores them in order to find the right combination. So let's examine the means of arriving at other alternatives, some of which we have already considered in different contexts.

Caucus

Take a break and get away for a few minutes to re-assess what has happened. Such reassessment may generate new insights and fresh ideas. In your caucus, try not to talk about walking out. This can become contagious and destroy productive thinking.

Recap

Sometimes when we recap both parties get a clearer perspective of their relative positions and are better able to decide whether to continue on the same path or to alter it. In either case, a recap tests whether any change is really possible.

The Doomsday Tactic

Discuss what the outcome will be if you don't negotiate. Describing the negative results of *not* negotiating can influence others to start up again. Talking about the self-defeating aspects of a failed negotiation may make your opponent realize that an impasse is to his disadvantage. The doomsday tactic may strike a sensitive note in otherwise deaf ears. However, be prepared for your opponent to disagree with your dire predictions and to respond that "Your crystal ball is cloudy."

Express How You Feel

As previously noted, expressing how you feel can result

in a fresh determination to work out a solution to the problem at hand. It often serves to liberate both parties from a viewpoint that the situation is hopeless.

Change the Subject

Introduce another issue, view, approach. Don't belabor the subject that has gotten both of you tied up in knots. Without actually sweeping the topic under the table, put it aside for a while and go on to something else that may become more productive. If the other party refuses to change subjects, explain that moving to other issues does not mean you are forgetting the unresolved ones. The cooling effect of letting go when a subject gets too hot can be very effective to the overall negotiation. It tends to circumvent overheating.

Attempt to Get an Agreement in Principle

Getting fundamental agreements in principle—such as "We agree that we must work out some kind of compromise," or "We are here to negotiate," or "We want to do business with each other," or "We need each other"— can sometimes bring parties back to the serious aspects of negotiation in recognition of fundamental common needs.

Get a Bridge-Issue Agreement

Most negotiations have built into them innocuous issues that are of little importance and can be easily agreed to.

Such agreement often breaks a deadlock. I recently read how a marriage counselor dealt with marriage disputes that were at an impasse by attempting to establish basic agreement between the parties on one relatively minor aspect of their life together. From here he would build on this point of agreement to reconcile touchier issues— the similarities and differences that led to conflict and discord in the marriage. Interestingly enough, more than one seminar attendee has questioned whether the material covered in our negotiating program would not be applicable in marriage counseling.

Take another example. In a certain labor dispute, the union demands are: (a) a 17 percent increase in salary, (b) greater retirement benefits, (c) more voice in management decisions that affect workers, (d) changes in grievance procedures, and (e) changes in the design or color of the uniforms supplied by the company because the present black uniform is "too depressing." In this example the last issue would probably be the bridge issue. Establishing an agreement there may very well result in a more relaxed attitude allowing for the kind of give-and-take that will generate agreement on the other issues more readily.

Discuss What Alternatives Remain

By redirecting the discussion from an impasse to what alternatives remain you can switch from a negative to a positive path. If the answer is that no alternatives remain, don't be discouraged unless you actually want the process to break down. Discouragement will give your opponent a golden opportunity to say good-bye. If you remain aware of the doomsday tactic, you may still be able to generate alternatives even if a first response to what alternatives remain is "none." Many answers exist to any problem. It requires persistence and creativity to find them. This, when coupled with fear, can be a foremost ingredient for problem solving.

Make Strategic Disclosures

In most negotiations each party knows something the other is not aware of. So negotiation to some extent becomes a "What do you know that I don't know?" process. Both parties are inevitably aware of this, yet frequently act quite in-the-know on all points. This can be very self-defeating.

When disclosures are made, they are usually received with enthusiasm, like a hung curve ball by a home-run hitter. During a deadlock, telling something unknown—especially if it can benefit the other party—usually gets quick attention and serves to start things going again in the right direction. Remember, though, if you do choose to disclose, do it incrementally and not by gut-spilling.

Ask a Hypothetical Question

The "what if" approach can be very effective when used at the right moment. But when considering this alternative, don't let your words get you into hot water by saying something that may be misinterpreted. Give some thought to structuring your question so that the meaning will be clear. Remember the prayer: "Lord, make my words sweet and tender for I may have to eat them tomorrow." Don't use these questions carelessly or too early, because individuals normally hear them as areas of possible "give." Premature use can lead to pressure for making early concessions.

Give or Get Empathy

We have all heard expressions like "I know how you feel," "I've been in your shoes," "I see your position, but my hands are tied by my company." Sometimes this expression of understanding posture can smooth the course of your conflict. Empathy can be given and gotten sincerely without endangering your position, particularly when you are negotiating as an agent for a principal, for it need not compromise your principal's objectives. But remember that if you do give empathy, the other party may later attempt to use it as a wedge, trying to enlist you, as it were, on its side. When that happens, stress the limitations of your position.

Try a Quick Close

Possibly your negotiation has come to an impasse because both of you have been jockeying for position. At this point, try for a quick close, such as, "Will you take $49,000 for it?" or "How about settling this at $10,000?" Although you may get a quick handshake acceptance, you should be prepared as well to get a quick rejection. Your opponent may also respond by asking why he should settle at the quick-close number. But whatever the reaction, you've gotten the negotiation temporarily out of the rut and moving.

Diagram Differences

Another worthwhile alternative in an impasse is to diagram the specific differences on a blackboard, flip chart, or piece of paper. Such diagrams often dramatically demonstrate that the differences separating the parties are slight. Visualization of how close agreement can be may lead to actual agreement. If you continue to verbalize your varying positions the result may be further separation. I have found in many arguments that the parties agree more often than disagree. That is the thing to get a focus on when an impasse has you locked into a concentration on the differences in points of contention. Diagram the differences in the context of the overall situation you're dealing with, and a realization often emerges that agreement is closer than you thought.

Give Something to Get Something

A deadlock can be broken by a compromise offer. Probably one of the most frequently asked questions in our seminars is when to make a compromise. That question may be answered by looking at the different reasons for making compromises: to get something, because it is conditional on something we have received or gotten, or because we are forced into it—as Winston Churchill said, "an appeaser is one who feeds a crocodile, hoping it will eat him last." Although it is sometimes thought to be very demeaning, the possibility of compromise is the essence of negotiation. When compromise means giving without getting, I think that indeed it is not very constructive. But where it means giving and getting, as I feel it must, then the outcome is positive.

Talk About Past and Future Needs

Many businessmen think about needs only in the present tense, even though the needs we have exist in the past and future as well. So when attempting to break a deadlock try to address yourself to needs other than just present ones. What will be the benefit of an agreement at a future time, if there seems to be no immediate perceived benefit? Or what past difficulty could have been avoided?

Use Past History and Good Association

If you have had favorable and productive dealings with your opponent in the past, the recollection of that may help get you together again. The approach is that since you both have worked together and solved similar problems or difficulties, why can't you do it once more? In many situations the answer is that you can. All that's required is a little more effort, support, cooperation, or compromise. Remember that trust and goodwill are not merely words to a negotiator. They are the backbone of the process. Therefore, when in a deadlock, returning to and reflecting on past periods of trust between you may spark the embers of goodwill.

Change Locations

In some instances, simply changing locations might save the negotiation. Getting away from the conference room or office and going to the manufacturing area, accounting department, or an engineering drawing board often results in a change of position as well as location, for now the parties must get up and walk, and, unless a conference area is provided, they will probably remain standing wherever they wind up. Negotiations conducted standing up tend to be shorter and more specific, and seem to get better interaction. I've always been a strong advocate of not sitting too long because I've seen behavior changes that were influenced by the resultant discomfort. Would you be supportive and cooperative if you were physically uncomfortable? For this reason, I always apply the ninety-minute principle in conducting seminars. Attendees are never required to stay in a sitting position for more than 90 minutes without stretching, or taking a coffee or lunch break. I learned a long time ago that when you extend this period for even another ten or fifteen minutes you run the risk of undermining all previous efforts.

Walk Out

I've saved this alternative for last merely because it should be employed only as a last resort. It doesn't take much creativity to get up and leave when things aren't going well. And if you do, remember that you may have to eat crow. Walking out may require you to come back and apologize or ask forgiveness. Unless you're pretty certain that walking out will jolt the negotiation into a new life, it's probably best not to do so. That's not to say that eating crow will kill you—many a successful negotiator has had the experience—but it isn't something to look forward to.

7

Strategy and Tactics

Strategy might be defined as the overall plan, approach, or concept that we have with respect to a negotiation; tactics as the step-by-step methods we use to implement the strategy. Sometimes strategy is tied to a single, specific tactic, and then the two coincide. But usually there is a clear distinction. Strategy and tactics are an inevitable result of planning your course through a negotiating situation. In addition, they are necessary because the other party will probably use them and you must be prepared to counter with your own. But neither the general strategy nor the specific tactics should be readily identifiable by your opponent or else they'll lose their punch. This is why, in negotiations where the parties know each other well, or where there is mutual trust and goodwill, few psychological tactics are used.

They are just too transparent and thus become self-defeating.

The tactics described below are psychological ploys that have been found effective in many a negotiation. They are, in effect, specialized tools that are helpful for a negotiator to know. Some of those that follow are tools you can consider for adoption. Others are ploys you may find being used against you. It's important that you cultivate an awareness of both types and learn to work them or counter them to your own advantage.

UNDERMINING

One party puts the other on the defensive and acts to keep him there. The individual employing the undermining tactic usually starts out by questioning you in a manner that verges on accusation: "Why didn't you do such and such?" "Why is your product so poor?" or "What's happened to your operation or service?" Then he continues to pepper you with negative statements or questions about your position, condition, or operation. The approach can be successful when one is in a strange position, with needs that are less pressing than an opponent's. The negative aspect of this tactic is that it antagonizes some people, causing them to pull back from concessions they might have been willing to make. People who have been made uncomfortable tend to be less compromising and cooperative.

The undermining approach works best when it is applied for brief periods, between which other tactics are used. My recommendation is that you don't lean on it too hard or too long unless you want to humiliate your opponent. And if that is the case, you should question why you even have to negotiate.

GOOD GUY–BAD GUY

The good guy–bad guy ploy is an internationally recognized tactic that requires at least a two-member team. It is a tactic frequently used—in modified form, of course—by police interrogators. The ploy is that one person behaves very emotionally and shouts, pounds tables, and uses four-letter words, while his team member/colleague/associate keeps a quieter profile. This balance is maintained for a specific period in order to shake up and unsettle the opponent. The range of positions shown can quickly establish that you intend to be tough and yet compromising.

The difficulty in using this tactic is the selection of the bad guy. Sometimes we select someone who plays the role so well that he doesn't want to give it up. When it's time for the good guy to take over, to come to the rescue, he finds it difficult because his companion doesn't want to leave the stage. Another problem in using this tactic is that it's sometimes too obvious. Some years ago I recall using it with an associate playing the bad guy. We were no more than ten minutes into our role-playing when our opponent said, "That's number four." We looked at each other and repeated, "number four?" "Yes," he said, "that's what we call the good guy–bad guy tactic. Please continue." There is nothing worse for a negotiator than to get caught with his tactics down.

A final word of warning. The disruptive force of the bad guy can sometimes trigger hostility, and where you might otherwise have found cooperation and support, you now find defensiveness. The tactic seems to work best when the negotiation appears destined to be a prolonged process and quick, easy solutions are sought.

WE'RE THE GREATEST

Some companies and individuals act as if they don't understand why you would dare question their integrity, quality, or record. They cite extraordinary past accomplishments and seem shocked that you disapprove of them. Several firms in the computer/technology business have continuously employed this tactic. It is effective when it's evident that the opposing party is impressed with you or your organization's reputation. From the other side, when it's used against you, don't succumb to a claim of "We're the greatest." Test it by having them tell you how they are going to stay on top. Take the attitude of "Yes, but what have you done for me lately?"

GREATER REWARDS

A very common tactic for getting compromise—usually most effective toward the end of a negotiation—is to promise greater rewards. Some have called it the "carrot principle." In application, an individual who has seriously been offering one unit of profit suddenly says, "Well, how about four?" in the hope that the possibility of greater stakes will motivate you to make concessions or at least think about them. This increase in potential profit or business is designed to act as a lever to get you to give.

When this tactic is used against you, my suggestion is to go along for the ride. Few individuals are prepared to commit themselves to more business. For them it is a test flight into the sky of possibility. So go along into the blue sky and swirl along with their high hopes. Entertain visions of what may be possible. Just don't confuse speculation with commitment. Usually the descent back to earth will bring you back to where you started.

INVOKING THE COMPETITION

To get a seller to reduce the price or give additional goodies, most buyers cite his competition. Few companies are in a noncompetitive field. The tactic is designed to get you to match the stated competitive situation. One response to this tactic that I've found to be very successful is what I call "the prodigal son." Rather than running down the quality or capability of competitors, respond by saying, "In the event you choose to do business with XYZ company and things don't work out to your satisfaction, we will be happy to do business with you"—meaning, come back to us, we will be waiting. Don't close any doors when someone subtly or firmly expresses a wish to go to another firm. Leave the door ajar for future entry. Do that explicitly and often you'll find the statement of intent to go with the competition was a test—the buyer is still interested in your product or service.

Even when you do use the "prodigal son" response, continue to argue for the order, use of your product, and so on. Don't let it appear as if you are willing to give up business easily. Don't concede to the competition until it's evident your own best offer is not acceptable. Then be graceful in admitting defeat. Your tact at this point leaves the door open to later business opportunities.

"I DON'T HAVE THE AUTHORITY"

Because most negotiations have a principal-and-agent relationship, the agent often uses this ploy in order to keep from being pinned down to settlement or agreement. It obviously is a very good strategy to go into a negotiation, get the other party to lay things out fully, and then leave because you are not able to make the final decision. It gives you time to formulate your strongest response. At a seminar in London an attendee stood up and said, "Mr. Calero, I negotiate all the labor contracts in the U.K. for my company. Do you think that our president should attend?" My response was, "Keep him the hell out!" He then turned to the person sitting next to him and said, "See, I told you so." Apparently he had advised his boss that it would be more advantageous for an agent to negotiate without the principal in attendance. This is an everyday tactic, effective in many situations. When buying an automobile, many times you hear the salesperson say, "Let me check this with the sales manager"; or the buyer say, "Let me see what my wife [or husband] thinks of it." Deferring in this way to another person is common the world over, and is meant to delay making a decision.

This tactic naturally cannot apply when you are clearly the principal and acting in your own behalf. And sometimes buying time this way is self-defeating. One of the saddest negotiating experiences in my life was when I used this tactic in Geneva. When window shopping in 1970 I saw a beautiful porcelain bust of King Tut, so much like the original death mask that it was unbelievable. The cost was $2,000, which at the time I considered a sum one didn't carelessly spend. After much thought and talk with the merchant I said, "I'll discuss this with my wife." When I next returned to the shop, the bust had been sold. Now, many years later, I'm still looking for that porcelain bust, and would be willing to pay many times the original price for it.

BIT-BY-BIT

In negotiations with contractors or others whose costs go into materials, labor, and subcontracting, the bit-by-bit tactic can be very effective. Rather than looking at total cost, each separate element is looked at individually with the intent of taking off the fat, much like a butcher trimming a steak or pork chop. In so doing, the result is more lean meat. We wind up with more substance than with grease.

Yet the experienced meat cutter knows that a certain amount of fat gives the meat a better flavor. So, to counter this tactic, tell the opponent what he will lose by trimming the "excess." In a contracting situation that can mean changes that affect such things as esthetics and standards of comfort that the buyer may not realize would be sacrificed. More than one home buyer, for example, has found that cutting "excess" in evaluating costs for a new home can result in use of fixtures that, while serviceable, are not what would have been preferred.

"IT'S NOT STANDARD!"

In our age of specialization, seemingly nothing is standard. If your opponent cries, "It's not a shelf item," you are supposed to appreciate the high price he just quoted because what you want has to be specially made. But there are few products or systems that are made up from scratch—the majority of them are put together from existing components. What makes them so-called specialty items is that the final product differs somewhat from those normally produced or sold. Pareto's Law of 80-20 certainly applies here: Approximately 80 percent of specialty products are made from items that are standard, while only 20 percent have to be specially made. So don't let this tactic deter you in your quest to get a better deal.

SELF-ADMONISHMENT

The ploy is to lay out in detail your own wrongdoings and responsibility in a situation that is proving difficult. It works better if you can add that you have learned something from the experience and have implemented procedures that will prevent a recurrence of whatever you did wrong. Most of us respect individuals who have the strength of character to say they were wrong, and we tend to ease up in our demands on them. Some negotiators take advantage of this reaction and use self-admonishment expertly. If the tactic is employed against you, let the negotiator spank himself but don't throw him a line by saying, "It wasn't all your fault" or "You couldn't help it." Hear him out and then simply go on. Self-admonishment is a short-lived tactic because it hurts too much to continue criticizing oneself. You will probably find that the tactic is dropped when you don't respond in the desired helping manner.

WET NOODLE

Have you ever attempted to push a wet noodle around? Some negotiators act like sodden noodles because they do not respond to any force or pressure. They negate action with inaction. It can be a very unsettling experience to tell someone something that is of great importance to you and then get absolutely no emotional or verbal response. Sometimes, it generates even greater emotional reaction on your part. One thing wet noodles are not usually prepared for is emotional involvement. Sometimes losing your temper or pounding on the table will get a "wet noodle's" attention. So if you can hook them into it by saying anything that will cause them to commit themselves, you've equalized the tactic. You have dried them out! Learn to observe the body-language clues these people give. These will aid you in identifying points on which you can push for reaction and probably get it.

"WHAT COULD BE WRONG?"

It sometimes happens that negotiators feign an innocent ignorance of a fact or situation that you feel requires explanation or remedy. We learn the value of this tactic early in life when caught in the act of taking something we are not supposed to have or doing something we ought not to do. Often avoiding a direct response to a question or remark about some difficulty is the characteristic means of maintaining an innocent demeanor. I recall an excellent example of this in a TV incident about a husband being discovered by his wife in bed with another woman. Husband and friend were both naked as the wife walked in and said, "Ralph, who is that woman in bed with you?" He responded, "You're home early, darling." She said, "Don't darling me, tell me what's going on!" The husband said, "Had a tough day, haven't you?" To which the wife replied, "Don't sweet-talk me, you creep!" While the dialog was taking place, both the husband and the bed mate were in the process of dressing. The wife angrily yelled, "This is it Ralph, no more!" As the other woman, now fully dressed, walked out of the room, Ralph queried, "What's for dinner?" The wife meekly remarked, "Spaghetti."

Feigning lack of responsibility or involvement puts the burden of pressing guilt on the other person. Instead of admitting compliance with an attitude or complicity in a deed or act, the tactic calls for skirting the point. It's often enough successful because confronting an opponent on a point of dishonesty or lack of forthrightness is uncomfortable and unsettling to many people. If this tactic of feigned ignorance or innocence is used against you, don't let your opponent off the hook.

"DO YOU REALLY WANT OUR BUSINESS?"

The "do you really want our business" tactic is used to get you to bend over backward by putting the burden of showing good faith—by compromising—on you. The test is one that requires thought, not impulsive reaction. So a hypothetical response such as "If I do, what will it cost me?" might be effective. That should get a debate under way to decide the merits or demerits of the situation. This tactic seldom works if the question—it's almost an ultimatum—is brought under scrutiny.

"IT'S NOT INDUSTRY PRACTICE"

The "it's not industry practice" tactic attempts to convince others that a particular practice should be accepted or rejected because the majority do so. I recall as a boy of nine stealing doughnuts from a bakery and then being caught. The owner gave me a lecture I never forgot. When he asked me, "Why did you steal those doughnuts?" I said, "Because the other kids do it." He quickly turned me around by saying: "Don't you want to be different?" That incident has been a lasting lesson.

Don't let anyone put you off with the words "It's industry practice" to justify his position. We had a swimming pool built in our home in California and the contractor advised us that the terms of payment were "forty-five percent after we dig, forty-five percent after gunite, and ten percent when the job is done." When I refused to agree to these terms, he responded that they were industry standards and showed me the payment clause in small print in the contract. Nonetheless, I insisted that the payment schedule be altered. After much fussing and a call to his office, we got a better payment arrangement that ensured that our swimming pool would be finished for the contractor to pull out his profit. Instead of 10 percent on the tail end, we got 25 percent.

DOOMSDAY

We've seen this tactic in another context. The soothsayer warns of impending doom unless you heed his advice. Obviously, the tactic is meant to frighten you into immediate action, usually beneficial to your opponent. Sometimes this is an effective tactic, because there are consequences to be considered, but very often it is used to intimidate. Remember that the future is not something that anyone can accurately predict. Some may come close to it, but how much that can be attributed to lucky guessing is only conjecture. Yet this tactic persists and we are bombarded with it in business and media advertising. "Your crystal ball is cloudy," is one of my responses to doomsday. Refuse to share your opponent's forecast and you'll force him to employ other arguments, which will probably result in an opening of alternatives. Of course he may also fall back on other tactics, which you also want to be alert to.

FUNNY MONEY

People are often very gullible when told what a good deal they're getting, especially when someone throws out percentages or bottom-line figures that sound stupendous. Organizations trying to attract the small investor to become his own boss do this especially well. In their sales pitch they claim that by investing a small amount of money and time the individual can push his income to astronomical sums. They fail to advise you of all the others attempting to do the same, except to cite instances of amazing success. Somehow the examples of a few who have made a success in the venture are used to convince you that everyone going into it will win. And a fair number of the success stories are inevitably difficult to verify. As others have said, "There is no free lunch." So don't accept just any facts or figures as absolutes. Snake oil salesmen are still around looking for buyers—and there are buyers.

QUICK CLOSE

We have already encountered the quick-close ploy as a means of breaking a deadlock. But the tactic can also be used at any time in a negotiation. It is mostly seen toward the end, although sometimes individuals try to button down the process rapidly by using it very early on. Words such as "Would you take fifty thousand dollars?" or "How about ten percent of the deal?" or "Let's split the difference and call it a day," are meant to close the gap between the parties very quickly. The danger is that the offer may be too arbitrary for either party to accept. For this reason, the tactic seems to work best when it is used for the purposes of testing or trial closing. Whether the offer is accepted or rejected, the response will help us gauge whether we are in the right ballpark and start looking to find the dugout for a final settlement. If the tactic is used on you, try repeating the offer. It may get the party making the offer to increase it or justify it. In either case, it puts the burden of selling on the other party.

If you're using the tactic, be careful you don't throw out an offer you'll have to renege on if accepted by your opponent. Be sure you have your own figures in order and, if you're an agent, that your quick-close is certain to be acceptable to the principal behind you.

FISHING

As anyone who has ever fished knows, sometimes you catch them and sometimes you don't. However, fishermen continue casting and are not easily discouraged. The same applies to negotiating. We go fishing for information about interests, needs, concerns, and so on. And like fishermen who get up early in the morning, we try this tactic in the early stages of the negotiation. It is sometimes called "feeling out the other party," or "testing the water," or "getting a temperature reading." Since it is not unusual for both parties to be fishing in the same spot and at the same time, it can be extremely entertaining to watch them both cast about while trying not to get their hooks snagged. At few other times are both parties more acutely aware of what's going on. If only this degree of awareness could continue throughout the balance of the process!

Fishing is necessary to establish guidelines. Like feedback received when courting, it tells you if you are heading in the right direction and how far to go. As one negotiator recently stated, "I don't mind the courtship in a negotiation because I know it leads to getting in bed with a deal."

8

Planning Your
Next Negotiation

Now that we've looked at the negotiating process from
several vantage points, it's time to put it all together in
a way that will help you plan your next negotiation.

PREPARATION

The common lament is this: "If only we had enough
time to prepare." No one ever thinks he has sufficient
time for all the necessary preparation, yet we are all expected to negotiate successfully. The purpose of this
section is to cover some specific areas of preparation
that we sometimes neglect or forget, and to learn how
to make better use of the time we do have. Although
we may all *want* more time, in fact we often have the
amount we *need*.

Preparation can be divided into the following general areas:

1. Anticipation of attitudes and behavior
2. Analysis of objectives and issues
3. Outside assistance
4. Composition of the negotiating team
5. Planning strategies and tactics
6. Leverage analysis (see pp. 26–27)
7. Compromises and fallback positions
8. Psychological factors
9. Use of visual aids
10. Postnegotiation analysis

The preparational phase need not necessarily follow the list as numbered, but at some time during preparation all of these factors should be considered for discussion and evaluation.

Anticipation of Attitudes and Behavior

In the military, this step would be called "know your enemy." Reflect on previous negotiations or meetings with the people who are to be involved. Know who attended; what demands were made; what was their attitude; where did it take place, etc. Using those dear friends, who, what , when, where, why, and how can be of great benefit.

When you may not have had previous experience with your opponents, it may be possible for you to contact a friend, business acquaintance, or colleague and ask about the behavior, conduct, and negotiating style of the people you are to deal with. Don't walk into a negotiation cold lest you be caught off guard by unexpected personalities and methods. One negotiator I recall had a habit of angrily exclaiming "we can always walk out" when he wanted to force concessions out of others. Anticipating that he might do this—and knowing it was merely a ploy—kept his opponent from conceding too much.

Sometimes your inquiry may lead you to predict only that the person will be unpredictable. But at least you will be prepared. Not planning how to cope with possible disruptions can derail the direction of your negotiation.

Also keep in mind that contrived behavior and feigned emotions are negotiators' tools. I strongly believe many successful negotiators would make good professional actors, for they must do a great deal of acting and improvising—especially if they have to "wing it" through a tough negotiation. When there is little time to prepare, a small amount of information and a weak position, then talent, experience, and acting ability are the keys to success.

Analysis of Objectives and Issues

The presentation of a general overview, an integral part of the negotiating ritual, should be an important consideration in your preparation. Once the basic opening overview has been decided, you should analyze what the specific issues are or may be. These usually fall into four categories:

1. Your issues or conditions as you see them
2. Their issues, sometimes differing from yours

3. Common issues affecting both parties
4. Hidden issues, which it may or may not be wise to bring out in the negotiation

After dividing the issues under these four heads, decide whether they are major or minor and whether their effect is short or long term. Obviously, you would like to trade off a minor short-term issue to settle a major long-term one. But it's hard to do this successfully unless you've defined the character of each issue first. Any further stratification of issues based on specific negotiating needs will be an additional asset to your objectives. This preparation is extremely important when you reach the stage of possible compromises or fallback positions. It is especially then that you want to be clear on the distinction between various issues.

Outside Assistance

In some negotiations, assistance may be required from attorneys, expert witnesses, or other highly qualified individuals. In your preparation, discuss whether the use of such people is advantageous. If it is, the person selected should be instructed as to which areas you wish him to discuss and which ones to stay out of.

In addition, test your witnesses as a lawyer might do, to see how they respond to stress, anger, intimidation, or other likely factors intended to neutralize them or their testimony. Do not bring in a witness who tends to get angry and confused when challenged.

Composition of the Negotiating Team

When your negotiations are part of a team effort, the choice and selection of members depends primarily on the nature of the negotiation. For example, if you are to discuss a major building construction contract with a prospective client, you certainly want to have designers, architects, and engineers who are working with you on the project to be on hand and ready to supply information relative to their areas of expertise. If the meeting is going to be a numbers session where details of costs, labor hours, subcontracting expenses, and the like will be the subjects, then your accounting personnel, budget manager, materials director, or purchasing agent should probably accompany you. And, finally, if the negotiation is going to deal with legal matters or possible problems therein, a legal counsel might be one of your team members.

There is no magic formula for the ideal number on a team. (Four members or fewer seem to be the ideal preferred by the majority of seminar attendees.) How they get along with each other, work together, and pick up each other's cues is of greater importance. In situations where backup team members are not required for provision of technical expertise, my own preference is for a two-member team. This provides the benefit of an added observer and idea generator, but keeps misunderstanding within the team to a minimum.

I strongly recommend that someone be appointed spokesman or chief negotiator, regardless of how many team members there are. In this way, you can ensure that the overall objectives and methodology of negotiating are consistent with the preparation and planning. Direction and purpose need some form of overall guidance. Few things are more frustrating than to deal with a group of individuals negotiating without leadership.

In our negotiating laboratory we can readily spot those who do not have much team negotiating experience. They usually speak out of turn, disrupt their team members' presentations, and in general contribute little to the successful outcome. These participants are used to negotiating in one-to-one situations where they ask and answer all the questions. They are not used to taking a back seat and find it very difficult to remain silent.

Teamwork can be highly productive. As we have said before, two heads *are* better than one. Two more eyes to see things you missed, two more ears to hear subtle messages not picked up by your antennae, and another brain to process the input data and give a readout to consider when evaluating your own assessment.

Planning Strategies and Tactics

Negotiators love to discuss favorite ploys and can recite the dates, times, and places they enjoyed phenomenal success using them. I think the best strategy or tactic is the one that gets the job done and allows both parties to leave with the feeling that the effort was mutually beneficial. Anything short of this may in the long run come back to haunt you.

When discussing what overall strategies or specific tactics to use, always keep the total effect in mind, not just the short-term achievement or objective. This will keep you from impulsively selecting a method that will win the battle but lose the war. Remember that winning an argument is for debaters, not negotiators. Someone once wrote, "How to make a point without making an enemy is important in settling conflicts." This certainly applies to negotiators.

Prepare all the tactics necessary to support your overall strategy but don't be compulsive about using them. The more people start to compromise, give to get, fall back, make proposals or offers, the less psychological tactics are used. I would say that roughly 80 percent of all tactics come into play before anything is offered or conceded. The period when both parties are vying for position, testing, and probing is when most tactics are used. When you get down to the fine strokes of working out a deal, pulling one too many tactics from your bag may blow the settlement.

Leverage Analysis

Although in the course of a negotiation you may find yourself having to devise a leverage factor to provide yourself an advantage in the negotiating process, most of the factors ought to be evident to you already. Review the list that appears on pages 26–27 for a review of what these are likely to include.

Compromises and Fallback Positions

If you think compromise will be necessary, prepare for it, always remembering that you want to get something in return. Consideration should be given to the reasons for and timing of such action. In other words, compromises and fallbacks from your original demands should be prepared with an objective in mind. They shouldn't be undertaken because you think it's always a good idea to compromise. That's not in your best interest. Sometimes when we act as our own agent—when we are the principal—we tend to make compromises rather quickly. In the same situation when acting as agent for another, we are more aware that we will be subjected to serious questioning, so hold out longer for our original objectives.

When considering the precise terms of a compromise offer, remember *never* to bracket it—never say, "I might be willing to knock off ten or fifteen percent." When others receive two figures they invariably take the one that benefits them the most. We say, "Don't give the other fellow a bracket option, but do get one yourself if possible."

Psychological Factors

Of all the aspects of negotiating, the psychology of dealing with others and how they react to conflict continues to be of great interest to all of us. If you understand what motivates people in conflict situations, you can plan your response rather than act on the spur of the moment. When individuals are faced with problems, they tend to follow certain behavioral patterns. It's as important to be as aware of the following six reactions to conflict in those who are your team members as it is to recognize them in your opponents.

1) Some negotiators withdraw, postpone, or try to circumvent a conflict situation by becoming very passive and nonassertive. Such behavior indicates that they regard the situation as hopeless: "Even if I became involved it wouldn't help matters." This pessimism is further motivated by a desire to avoid responsibility for possible failure.

2) Not infrequently a negotiator will indicate he wants to see the situation handled by someone else. Conflict makes him uncomfortable, so he asks that matters be turned over to a third party who will work out the differences. Some negotiators readily accede to this call for a referee, especially when the conflict seems impossible to resolve and they have reached a high level of anxiety and frustration. Of course, turning your conflict over to a mediator or arbitrator may become necessary. But before you do so, make sure you have exhausted all other alternatives.

3) Some negotiators will continue to deny that any difficulty exists. In this, they are like Pollyanna, a little girl who never saw anything in a negative light. Her main hang-up was that she didn't like to face reality. At least those who withdraw or turn matters over to others are

aware of a conflict's existence. Only such awareness will keep the negotiation going. Refusal to admit to conflict makes it impossible to resolve conflict.

4) The negotiator who says "Let's negotiate" or "Let's work out a compromise" shows a combination of assertiveness and cooperation. Those who use this approach feel that the situation can be resolved through a win-win solution and that conflict should not undermine the relationship. Rather, they see it as very stimulating in generating creative alternatives. Conflict for this type of individual is not frightening or disruptive, but is seen as a challenge. He doesn't actively seek out problems, but readily accepts and deals with them.

5) The negotiator with a "yield and surrender" attitude betrays a total subordination of wishes, needs, goals, and objectives to someone else. The intention appears to be to avoid conflict so as to maintain some kind of relationship at any costs—even loss of self-respect. This approach is sometimes used when an individual feels he is losing or wrong. Rather than fight, he switches.

6) The "top dog" negotiator uses intimidation, dominance, and control to pursue his goals—usually at the expense of the other party. There is generally little attempt to achieve any compromise. Getting is the word; giving is unknown. Those most easily influenced by this person are noncompetitive individuals who find it very difficult to argue. Examples abound in history of leaders who relied primarily on this method for handling conflict. Hitler and Mussolini in particular shared this characteristic approach when dealing with others.

Use of Visual Aids

During preparation, ask if such material will be or should be used. If the answer is affirmative, then thought should be given to how to make the best presentation.

Apart from movies, overhead projectors, or slide projectors, visual aids fall basically into two categories, prepared or developed.

Prepared visual aids are designed, often by professional graphic artists, to illustrate everything from sales curves to organizational responsibilities. Such aids are carefully thought out and the details analyzed long before they reach the drawing board of the person who will put them in visual form. This type of aid is used to better demonstrate a point, as a persuasive device, and for purposes of clarity. Regardless of why they are used, visual aids are supposed to reinforce our position.

In the *developed visual aid,* no previous artwork is required. Although the amount of time needed for preparing the data is essentially the same, the purpose of using the developed visual aid is different. It is used to impress, overwhelm, and influence other parties by demonstrating that your knowledge is so extensive you don't need to resort to notes. Few moments in a negotiation are more impressive than when a person gets up from the table, goes to a blackboard or flip chart, and proceeds to lay out conditions, situations, financial accounting, sales figures, without the apparent benefit of written material.

The technique of using a developed visual aid works

best when the individual has good recall. To the observer, the person writing or drawing is merely referring to his memory. But, if he has planned properly, he is actually doing something that was worked out to the smallest detail beforehand.

A newspaper story concerning a very important malpractice case best illustrates this. A surgeon was being sued by one of his patients for malpractice in a heart-bypass operation. The attorneys for the plaintiff and defendant were also medical doctors, and prepared to enter discussion on any aspect of the law or the specific operation performed. The defense attorney had spent two weeks drawing the heart and all the arteries leading to it, plus other medical illustrations meant to describe the operation. When he got up in court, he deftly drew the heart in exact proportion. (He later claimed he had drawn it five hundred times in preparing for the trial.) When he described what his client did in surgery, he drew complex lines and curves that all seemed to fall into place. Later, the plaintiff's attorney admitted he had never seen anyone in a courtroom illustrate something quite that well. The developed visual aids were so impressive that a counter-argument was difficult to generate. Not only was the opposing attorney surprised but the jury and judge sat in awe at this artist in the courtroom who was so completely in control and in command of the situation.

Beyond the need for prior practice, an important lesson to be learned from this story is that you should go to the board as a coach and not as a scribe. The coach controls what is taking place and speaks as he illustrates.

The scribe is not in control and puts down what others have told him to record or illustrate. This major difference in role and function should not be forgotten.

Post-Negotiation Analysis

Doing your homework is not only a matter of preparing for the negotiation itself, but also of planning a post-negotiation analysis session. Such a session will help you determine the reasons for success or failure—which will certainly aid you in the future. But more important, it will indicate to you whether the deal will hold together. Negotiations, as we have seen, don't end with the handshake or signing of the agreement. It's only when the agreement has to be implemented that the process gets under way. So make plans to sit down with your negotiating team members, if there are any, and discuss what you did, what you got, what happened, and what impact the settlement may have.

It is far easier for the post-negotiation analysis to be made when there is more than one person on your side, because two or more generate interaction about what happened. When only one person is involved, it is sometimes rather difficult to write down for file and reference purposes what occurred. Individuals who are flushed with the feeling of success or depressed and worried by failure seldom like to transfer these feelings to paper. But most don't mind talking about it.

My recommendation for planning to cover this important aspect of the negotiating process is to prepare to take a cassette recorder with you, so that directly after the session is over, you can dictate all the post-negotiation information you and/or your team members believe is important for the records. Subsequently, you need only pop the tape into the recorder to get instant recall of what your feelings were immediately after the negotiation. A colleague of mine does this religiously. He likes it for review, twenty-four to forty-eight hours after the emotional aspects of the negotiation have subsided. At this time, he feels objective reasoning can be applied to the results, and that any potential sore spots can be identified and treated immediately, instead of having them fester and become dangerous.

THE STEP AFTER PLANNING—GETTING YOUR NEGOTIATIONS STARTED

In our seminar profiles we find some people claiming that one of the most disliked things about negotiations is getting them under way. Others easily take to starting and find no difficulty in getting the sessions rolling.

How the negotiation begins is important because it creates either a negative or a positive atmosphere that is likely to influence the ultimate outcome. An opening should convey positive feelings about working toward meeting mutual needs, a concern for remedial action, a general attitude of seeking out and discussing alternatives, and enthusiasm about being able to reach a settlement. This will surely be successful more often than an opening that features confrontation, threats, or intimidation. However, your attitude, even when 100 percent positive, should not be taken to mean that you will compromise just for the sake of an agreement. Instead, what should be clear is that you seek options and alternatives in order to reach conclusions.

You may plan to create an initial atmosphere different from the one you want to wind up with. For example, you may decide to stress the distance between respective initial positions. The intent is that once the later changes have moved both sides toward a mutually acceptable compromise, the enthusiasm generated is greater than it would have been had the sides been closer at the outset. This requires nursing the situation a lot in order to make the switch. Sometimes, although you want to make an adjustment, feelings have become so deep-seated that a change in atmosphere becomes very difficult to achieve. The parties concerned have solidified positions to the point of making it impossible to change directions.

In working to establish a favorable opening atmosphere, it is best to concentrate on operating from a state of mind that is not clouded with emotional reactions, whether to the issues at hand or to the opposing party. Success in negotiation requires learning the value of maintaining control, particularly when dealing with those who may be impatient or short-tempered.

As far as getting the negotiating environment set, select the time, location, and seating arrangement that satisfies both parties' needs. Psychological advantages to be gained here are generally minimal.

Negotiation Starting Positions

If you visualize the negotiating process as a track course to be run, you can view negotiators starting in lanes of behavior that would be illustrated as below:

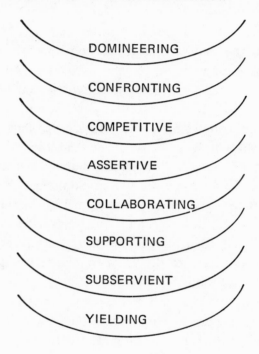

Note that I've placed the domineering runner in the inside position, which is the shortest distance around the track. However, unlike runners, negotiators may start in any lane of their choice and change as often as they wish. We have all seen negotiators start by elbowing each other for favorable positions on the inside lane and then winding up by shaking hands in one of the outside lanes.

The purpose of this illustration is to increase your awareness of the different behavioral choices available to all of us when we start negotiating. But don't carry the analogy too far. Unlike runners in a race, who finish in staggered positions, negotiators try to break the finish line fairly close together, so as to achieve a feeling that the race was won by all involved. Remember also that negotiation is not a process to be dashed through for quick victory. The best progress is that which is consistent, directional, and controlled.

9

Developing Your
Negotiating Skills

We have emphasized throughout this book that the individual who has the ability to see what's going on will hold an advantage. This ability is not an inherent gift; it must be cultivated, nurtured, and developed.

IMPROVING YOUR AWARENESS

To increase your awareness in the negotiating process, start by daily observing things around you that you normally disregard—for example, what clothes people are wearing and the approximate size, wall colors, floor covering, and furniture in a room you enter. The exercise can be expanded to include a myriad of other seemingly trivial observations.

With this sort of conditioning, you will find that at

your next negotiation, from the moment you or others enter a room you will automatically be making observations that will later be beneficial. Notice, for example, that individuals usually enter for an important meeting by buttoning their coats, as if to present the best picture of themselves. Also note that the senior negotiator is usually the first one across the threshold and normally carries the fewest documents. The "gun-bearers" follow with the tab runs or the stacks of records that are supposed to impress you. When everyone is seated and introductions have been made, observe that the person who will do most of the initial speaking tends to lean forward in his chair, while others on his team sit back waiting their turn.

I can best demonstrate what is useful to notice by following the negotiating process through three stages.

Stage 1: Developing the Climate

After assessing hundreds of videotaped buy-sell negotiating situations, we find that the seller tends to sit leaning forward somewhat on the edge of his chair; the buyer sits back and more upright. The seller's hands will be on the table, although often in movement, as he tries to convince, persuade, or influence the buyer, who is likely to be sitting with his arms crossed.

Three characteristic positions of the feet appear during this stage: (1) feet flat on the floor; (2) crossed or "locked" at the ankles; (3) in a spinster's position— back under the chair and raised on the toes. The seller, who has to be very aggressive, enthusiastic, or anxious, tends to be, as the expression goes, "on his toes"—that is, with heels raised as if about to start a race. The buyer, who for the moment takes a neutral stance, sits with both feet flat on the floor. Finally, persons who are holding back, taking a wait-and-see, or a don't-get-involved position, often adopt the locked-ankles posture. To verify this, look around at the next meeting you attend and notice that those who are contributing most tend to be leaning forward and generally don't have their ankles locked, while the less involved are sitting back with ankles crossed.

Stage 2: Conflict

This is where we usually spend the most time as we hammer out our differences. And some specific non-verbal gestures and movement can also be recognized here.

It is very significant in negotiations to see who is the first party to move away from the table. This usually signals the beginning of the conflict phase. Backing off is a dynamic illustration of the sense of distance experienced by either party. When individuals are at the greatest physical distance from each other, they usually are also far apart with regard to coming to terms. It is also very prevalent during the conflict stage for both parties to have their arms crossed. And they may both cross their legs in a backward movement. In a buy-sell situation, this is likely to be evident when the parties are far apart on price or on terms of payment.

From these relative positions the individuals may

move forward or sideways, stand up, walk around, or again move away until they finally reach the last phase.

Stage 3: Agreement-Settlement

The most positive phase of a negotiation is when the parties are both leaning forward, hands on the table, and sitting on the edges of their chairs. The expression "They're getting together" as opposed to "They're far apart" applies in this phase. Their gestures and postures clearly signal "We're close to a deal," or "We've just concluded an agreement."

The nonverbal signals noted above may assist you in recognizing the various stages of the negotiating process. Awareness is a necessary asset for every negotiator. The more we *see*, the more we understand. The more we understand, the more we can deal with.

INCREASING YOUR CREATIVE POTENTIAL

Jacob Bronowski, in his book *The Ascent of Man*, describes a conversation during World War II with his friend, the mathematical genius Johnny von Neumann. Bronowski asked, "You mean the theory of games is like chess?" "No. No," von Neumann said, "Chess is not a game. Chess is a well-defined form of computation. You may not be able to work out the answer, but in theory there must be a solution." Von Neumann went on to say that "real life consists of bluffing, of little tactics of deception, of asking yourself what is the other man going to think I mean to do."[1]

Negotiation incorporates elements common to this view of both chess and life. It is predicated on there being a solution—albeit one that allows both parties to appear as winners. And it involves a continual interaction between the parties that features tactics and attempts to anticipate another's reaction to what you are going to do. It is also characterized by reliance on creative ability to come up with answers and results.

Edward de Bono is an author who has written most perceptively about creative thinking. His books *Lateral Thinking*,[2] *Practical Thinking*,[3] *New Think*[4] and *PO: Beyond Yes and No*[5] are easy to read and understand and the practice exercises well worth doing. I strongly recommend de Bono's works for developing your creative potential. Here are some tips taken both from de Bono and from my own experience in the negotiating laboratory.

Juxtaposition

Try to juxtapose facts, observations, or whatever information is available, to come up with different views.

---

1. J. Bronowski, *The Ascent of Man* (Boston: Little, Brown, 1973), p. 432.
2. Edward de Bono, *The Use of Lateral Thinking* (London: Pelican Books, 1971).
3. de Bono, *Practical Thinking* (London: Pelican Books, 1976).
4. de Bono, *New Think* (New York: Avon, 1971).
5. de Bono, *PO: Beyond Yes and No* (London: Pelican Books, 1973).

This is one way to generate creative alternatives in negotiating.

In *How to Read a Person Like a Book* my co-author and I discussed the types of illustrations to use. We considered line drawings by an artist to show gestures and postures, but rejected this, feeling that the artist's esthetic concerns might distort what we wanted. Then we thought of using newspaper and magazine photographs of well-known personalities, but decided against that because of the amount of time required to receive approval from each individual before publishing the photo. Then we discussed using models to pose for photographs that would convey the various gestures, postures, and facial expressions we wanted to demonstrate. This also was not appropriate because it would look posed to the reader and therefore not realistic. Finally, by juxtaposing alternatives, we came up with a fourth: to select photos from news sources and then trace the forms, thus ending up with a line drawing. I added beards, mustaches, glasses, and so on, to disguise the celebrity. The result was a series of drawings that realistically depicted people being themselves and nonverbally communicating their feelings.

I have since used the juxtaposition approach in many other situations to come up with additional options. It is simple once you get used to doing it. Winston Churchill's creative wit was full of juxtapositions, such as when a British admiral radioed him, saying that if his task force continued to follow the *Bismarck* they would run out of fuel. When the admiral requested permission to return to base for refueling, Churchill simply responded, "Continue to follow—we'll tow you home."

Multiple Answers

When we have to come up with answers, we usually stop seeking after the first solution is at hand. It is almost as if we believe that the first answer provides the *only* way, instead of just *one* way to solve a problem. There is no limit to how many ways exist to do something or solve a problem. Providing we have time, we should continue to seek other methods of working out a solution and then select the best one to use. As de Bono states: "The search for alternative ways of looking at things is not natural. The natural tendency of the mind is to become impressed by the most probable interpretation, and then to proceed from that."[6]

Imagination

It has often been said that imagination and creativity are related, so let's see how we can become more imaginative. Imagination refers literally to our ability to form mental pictures, which we do in a way that is not clearly understood by researchers. Nevertheless, not everybody seems to have the inherent ability to form these mental images easily. To test yourself, close your eyes and picture a sailboat in choppy waters with a drunken sailor trying desperately to control the sails. If you find it's

6. de Bono, *Lateral Thinking* (London: Pelican Books, 1971), p. 79.

not easy, you may want to practice generating mental images.

As you try generating mental pictures, the exercise will become easier and the result visually more detailed with each effort. When you have a handle on this phase of imagination, add to it the ability to anticipate things, and empathy for what others are feeling. You will then be in a state to imagine things that may happen and to imagine others' reactions. With those factors put together, you're well on your way to becoming more creative.

Alertness to Indirect Approaches

B. H. Liddell Hart's book *Strategy* is a fascinating account of military campaigns, from the Greek wars of Epaminondas, Philip of Macedon, and Alexander the Great to the Arab-Israeli War of 1948–49.[7] The way generals plan their campaigns can often provide helpful hints for the negotiator. Liddell Hart constantly refers to "indirect approaches"—that is, through the use of imagination doing the unexpected and being where you were not expected or "supposed" to be. In negotiation, we sometimes refer to this as keeping others off balance. *Strategy* is excellent reading material for those who want to extend their creative potential. Although the examples are purely military, it's easy to make the transition from one field to the other. Liddell Hart's statement, "no man can exactly calculate the capacity

---

7. B.H. Liddell Hart, *Strategy* (New York: Signet Books, 1974).

of human genius and stupidity nor the incapacity of will,"[8] applies not only to warfare but to the negotiating table.

Group Creativity

Like many others, I have been exposed to group situations in which we were expected to come up with solutions and answers to specific problem circumstances. This "brainstorming" exercise is always based on the premise that two heads are better than one. The exercises were fun and I learned a great deal about negotiating in these sessions. How much each one of the participants improved his creative quotient was not measured and probably couldn't be. But I did come away from such groups understanding that creativity does not take up residence in only one house. Some of the participants were obviously more creative than others, although they may not have been any more intelligent. It's now obvious to me that another method of improving creative potential is to get together with others and follow a programmed approach to problem solving. The approach I prefer is that outlined by William J. Gordon in his book *Synectics:*[9]

1. Identify and understand the problem.
2. Collect relevant information.
3. Mull it over.
4. Speculate.

8. Ibid., p. 323.
9. William J. Gordon, *Synectics* (New York: Collier Books, 1968), p. 15.

5. Develop ideas.
6. Select the best idea.
7. Implement it.

In a group context this works extremely well.

Creativity in Dreams

Supposedly many of our real-life dilemmas are solved in our dream sequences. I can recall several instances in which ideas that were later applied to nagging problems came to me while I was sleeping. If dreams are such storehouses of creativity, how can we use them efficiently? Patricia Garfield's *Creative Dreaming* outlines methods and techniques for us to use.[10] Dr. Garfield stresses the use of prior programming, which she calls "dream incubations." To obtain creative answers in dreams, she recommends these three steps: (1) Clearly formulate the desired dream; (2) accept the fact that it is possible to induce dreams; (3) concentrate your attention patiently and persistently on the desired dream. I highly recommend Dr. Garfield's book as an aid in opening up an area of creativity that has great potential for everyone.

The Opposite Approach

Reverse psychology has been used successfully in some negotiating situations but has backfired in others. Those who have been burned will attest to the danger involved.

10. Patricia Garfield, Ph.D., *Creative Dreaming* (New York: Simon & Schuster, 1975).

Although Dr. Allen Fay, in his book *Making Things Better by Making Them Worse*,[11] probably doesn't realize it, he cites many negotiating examples when he suggests taking an opposite approach—which he calls "paradoxical therapy." Since creativity requires looking at everything from as many angles as possible, unexpectedly taking a position that accentuates the circumstances of a problem situation can lead to either the generation of new ideas or to a clearer realization of the nature of the issues that are proving difficult for the negotiators. An example in Dr. Fay's book is that of a wife who wanted her husband to take out the garbage. He constantly forgot, and they continually fought about it. One day she said, "Gee! That garbage really looks attractive near the door. Let's leave it there. I think it gives the kitchen a rather elegant atmosphere." The husband, amused, took the garbage out.

Concentration

Albert Einstein was supposed to be so good at concentrating that he sometimes forgot where he was or had been. The story about him meeting a student near the cafeteria is a good example. After discussing a class-related problem with Dr. Einstein, the student started to walk away and was stopped when Einstein asked, "Which way was I walking when you stopped to talk to me?" The student asked what difference it made,

11. Allen Fay, M.D., *Making Things Better by Making them Worse* (New York: Hawthorn, 1977).

and Einstein responded, "If I was walking towards the cafeteria it meant I was on my way to lunch. On the other hand, if I was walking away from it, it means that I've already eaten my lunch."

Concentration has been described as the "elimination of all images foreign to a train of thought."[12] My observations reveal that negotiators who possess powers of concentration also seldom miss what's happening. They tend to be good listeners as well, which implies that concentration can be external and internal. Great thinkers like Einstein use a lot of internal concentration when attempting to find solutions to problems. However, in negotiating situations, we often have to concentrate on external matters and block out the internal. The mind seems to have an outward-inward capacity for concentration, and we can turn it in the direction we want our attention to flow.

To test how much concentration improves our powers of observation, I once asked twelve people in a seminar to pick a lemon out of a bag. Next, each was to spend five minutes carefully studying the shape, texture, and color. After this, they all put their lemons back into the bag. Then I dumped all the lemons on a table. Each one was told to reclaim the lemon he had studied. Each participant picked up the one he believed to be his and no squabble followed. Through concentration they were able to make distinctions that they probably would not have made in a more conventional situation. Try this

12. Ernest Dimmet, *The Art of Thinking* (New York: Simon & Schuster, 1928) p. 93.

exercise at a small social or family gathering and amaze people by showing them how well they can concentrate and improve their powers of observation.

Memory

There are three things I will always forget. Names, faces—the third I can't remember.

—ITALO SVEVO

The creative process requires the ability to recall information, so improving our memory system is another factor in developing our potential. Ongoing brain research has acquired a considerable amount of knowledge of how human beings retain data, and of the feedback process. There are many different memory courses, both in books and lecture form, that can help us to recall names, faces, and other things we often can't remember. I recommend taking advantage of those that might improve retention abilities if you're concerned to get more remembered information out of your personal biological computer.

Association

An idea is a feat of association.

—ROBERT FROST

One of the most remarkable characteristics of human beings is the ability to make mental associations—to connect one thought or observation with another in such a way as to establish a relationship between them.

The process can be convergent or divergent. It can synthesize two thoughts into a common association, or it can make two thoughts bond with two more separate thoughts. In illustration they might look like this.

Successful negotiators I know are marked by their abilities to establish logical relationships between disparate facts (convergence) and to propose alternatives arising from a single situation (divergence).

To improve your associative capability, spend a few moments each day doing what I call free-wheeling association exercises. Take a word, concept, or image and let your mind register whatever connections it might make with anything. Let the first thought out, as in psychological word association exercises, and don't attempt to block any subsequent thoughts, no matter how ridiculous. This helped me recently when I tried to solve a gardening problem. We had several low spots in our lawn that became puddles after each rain. I had thought of leveling the depressions with extra soil or digging deeper and filling the holes with rocks for drainage. Yet somehow I felt there were other possibilities. During a free-wheeling session with myself, I visualized a simple garden hose placed so as to act as a conduit draining off the excess water. The next rain, I tried it and it worked perfectly.

Or take the following example from an actual negotiating situation: An author's agent stressed his client's requirement for an increased advance for the author's second book, because the author required additional funds to research the subject he was treating in depth. The publisher, feeling that the market potential for the second book was not really greater than that for the first book, resisted the agent's demand, feeling that the additional advance monies requested probably would not be recouped in a subsequent larger sale. The editor, who wished to sign the book because he thought it a good project, but who was constrained by the company's decision to keep the advance amount at the previous figure, considered this seeming impasse and arrived at a compromise solution that met the needs of both parties. Ordinarily publisher's advance payments are made in two installments: 50 percent on signing of the book contract and 50 percent on delivery of the completed manuscript. The agent's demand was for a $20,000 advance; the publisher insisted on holding the line at a $15,000 advance. The editor won agreement from both agent and publisher for a division of the advance monies so that the author would receive a $10,000 initial advance, providing up front the added funds deemed necessary for the research costs, then take a smaller $5,000 advance on delivery of the completed manuscript. In addition he won for the author a somewhat improved royalty schedule, so that if in fact the book outperformed its predecessor, an added benefit would accrue to the author. The needs and convictions of both parties were acknowledged in a compromise characterized in this case by convergent thinking.

An associative ability is one of the most important components of creativity. As novelist William Plomer observed, "It is the function of creative men to perceive the relations between thoughts, or things, or forms of expression that may seem utterly different, and to be able to combine them into some new forms—the power to connect the seemingly unconnected."[13]

---

13. Quoted by Dr. Laurence J. Peter, *Peter's Quotations* (New York: Morrow, 1977).

10

Profile
Questionnaire Response

The following is the result of our research findings relative to the 36 questions you were requested to answer in the introduction. We emphasize that there are no absolutely right or wrong answers to these questions because negotiating situations differ.

In comparing your responses with our findings, always think about your *overall* perception of the negotiating process. Is it idealistic or too skeptical? Overly naïve or too cynical? The purpose is to gauge your awareness of the process and allow you to become more successful as a negotiator.

1. When people disagree with your views or position do you try to convince them?

Very often we find negotiators attempting to convince others who disagree with them. This clash of positions or views seems to shift negotiating to the level of debating, as the negotiator tries through use of superior logic to get others to agree. Some negotiators go to great lengths to draw out examples to support their views. Whether logical or absurd, they seldom work because the other party usually responds with "By the same token . . ." or "That's like saying . . ." or, "On the other hand," and manages to squeeze out his particular example to refute the first. Although sometimes there are points to be debated, negotiation is not a process to prove one party more right or better than the other. It is rather one of coming to agreement while recognizing the different needs and viewpoints of the involved parties. Turning a negotiation into a debate generally results in lessening the likelihood of success.

2. When conflict exists between two parties, do you feel like compromising in order to resolve the dispute?

Conflict by itself seldom inspires individuals to compromise. Rather, it often hardens their positions and sometimes makes them more inflexible. What conflict accomplishes is the realization that objectives are not going to be easy to achieve, that their achievement requires work, patience, and creativity. To this end, successful negotiators seldom compromise just because of conflict. They normally compromise when they see the conflict subsiding and the possibility of a give-get situation in sight.

3. Do you believe that your usual preparations for a negotiation are adequate?

The motto "You can't be successful without doing your homework" certainly applies here. Yet "sometimes" is the answer given as much as "often" or "almost always." There are negotiations that are planned well in advance—as for a labor contract due to expire in three or six months—which allow us the necessary preparation. However, many negotiations occur as a result of something unexpected: some unforeseen accident, overnight change, notification of bad news. In situations such as these, we make whatever preparation we have time for and "wing it" from there. I've met some very successful negotiators who believe their accomplishments were based on being able to adjust to whatever took place *because of* lack of preparation. They weren't locked into a pre-established way of approaching problems that came up. It shows supreme confidence in negotiating when, given few facts and details, and a sketchy patchwork of objectives, issues, strategy and tactics, you still believe you'll be successful. As we said earlier, optimism is an element of success.

4. Do you believe that the person with the most facts will eventually be successful in a negotiation?

It still amazes me to meet the individuals who believe facts will change others' views. If your answer was "sometimes," "often," or "almost always," you have a surprise in store. Seldom do facts bring about success. Many negotiators seem to have a notion that facts were created not to be believed but to be disputed. Facts are argued, contradicted, confirmed, denied, established, or refuted, and finally—maybe—agreed to.

Further, in many negotiations the individuals who bring along the most facts prompt the greatest amount of defensiveness on the other side. So much of what people conceive as fact is so influenced by belief systems and personal feelings that facts others can prove or demonstrate are likely to be ignored. My recommendation is not to place too high a priority on establishment of facts as a measure of your success. But do remember that facts *may* influence individuals to rethink a position and then narrow the distance between you. A favorite statement of mine is, "You may not agree with the information I'm going to cover; however, I ask you to listen to it first before rejecting it."

5. Once you have decided what your objectives are, do you change them during the course of negotiating?

Negotiators seldom change their objectives during the course of negotiating. This is especially true for those who have had sufficient time to prepare their objectives. Even many who have not had time stick to their initial positions and resist change. When changes occur, it usually is a result of a new meeting or a caucus, or because new supportive information or behavior softens your position. When tough resistance starts to melt and shows an undercoat of giving, we sometimes are led to change our objectives. But this is just when we should remember our objectives and try to achieve them, instead of lowering them. The aspiration level of many negotiators is tested here, and those that pass are the ones who do not alter their objectives.

When objectives clash to the extent of causing an impasse, both parties may do well to rethink their strategy, tactics, issues, and objectives before changing them. At this point a caucus, adjournment for the day, or going to lunch or dinner is recommended, rather than switching objectives during the negotiation.

6. Is it possible for both parties in a negotiation to win?

Often both parties can leave a negotiation with the feeling that they won something. As we remarked earlier in this book, objectives differ and each side to a negotiation makes its own assessment of gain or loss. So win-win situations are often possible and realized. However, there are also situations when individuals on both sides leave feeling they lost or didn't achieve anything. And then there are those negotiations where one side clearly feels taken advantage of. This win-lose outcome often sets up target practice for the side that lost—with the side that won as the target. The subsequent potshots will eventually convince the winner that the victory gained was not so sweet. If negotiations are to proceed smoothly and the parties are to comply with the settlement, then both sides must have a feeling of getting something that they want. Otherwise, an atmosphere will develop where any compromise made will not be kept.

7. Do individuals who negotiate play games?

The situations set out by Eric Berne in his book *Games People Play* also apply to negotiators, who, after all, are also people. Negotiators often play games. For those of you who answered "almost always," have faith—there are a few negotiators who shy away from playing psychological games, and maybe you'll encounter one some day.

The games negotiators play are usually very unstructured and often go unnoticed even by the players. If someone accuses you of playing games, nine times out of ten you would respond, "I'm not." Our observations are that negotiators often play games, but seldom admit it.

8. Do these games negatively influence the negotiation?

Self-defeating games such as "gotcha," where one attempts to put another in a position of inferiority or to strip him of self-respect, sometimes have a negative influence on the process. However, the majority of games are expected, played, countered, and sometimes thoroughly enjoyed. Although at first a game may appear to take unfair advantage of the opponent, in the end each party knows that both have to get something out of the process. So usually even if they don't start out with a win-win strategy, they wind up that way.

9. When your opponent's strategy is to play games with you, do you counter with your own games?

As noted above, when the other party does play games, individuals often counter with their own.

10. Do you prepare written questions before negotiating?

Negotiators seldom prepare written questions prior to an actual negotiation. In asking this question for fourteen years, I've received a yes response from only 10 percent of my seminar attendees. Ninety percent of them admitted that in their preparation they never wrote out questions to be asked. It seems to me a consequence that the majority of questions that are asked are spontaneous and often poorly worded. This in turn causes problems in communication—further disagreement and sometimes greater conflict. My recommendation for all who negotiate is to write down at least five questions they would like to ask during the process. The discipline, once started, becomes a good habit with rewarding results.

11. Do your questions cause anxiety when asked?

Questions often cause anxiety in negotiations. The more poorly worded a question is, the greater the anxiety. The responsive chord is always in the receiver and not the sender, and questions do give rise to fear, doubt, and similar negative feelings.

12. Is the person asking the most questions in control?

Again, it has been surprising to find that negotiators don't ask very many questions. They do, however, make a great number of statements that are sometimes responded to as if they had been questions. When questions are asked, the person asking the most is sometimes in control. This is most often the case with the negotiator for a regulatory bureau who proceeds to pepper you with questions in order to put you on the defensive. In that situation, he often tends to control the flow and direction of the negotiation.

13. Can a caucus or adjournment be taken as a weakness?

A caucus or adjournment can sometimes be taken as a weakness. This is especially true of an early caucus, which might signal lack of preparation, underestimating the other party's position, or reliance on an assumption incorrectly made. The caucus that is appropriately timed is not viewed as a weakness. It is usually seen as a break to develop new strategy and techniques, formulate new positions, or prepare compromises.

14. Is a caucus an effective procedure?

Calling a caucus is often a good procedure. It allows your team to regroup, prepare new proposals, evaluate offers made. It also can be of benefit for your negotiating team to ask for a recess not because you need it, but because the other team evidently needs it and yet for some reason hasn't called for one. In this instance it benefits both parties.

15. *Should illogical approaches be used?*

It is sometimes very worthwhile to develop illogical approaches because they cause the other party to review its own logic. This can sometimes cause illogical positions and approaches on the other side to stand out more clearly. But often negotiators, to make a point, will rely on analogies or examples that are not only illogical but also inappropriate. Yet they continue to use them for purposes of influencing their opponent. A comical aspect of this is that *these* illogical examples will often be countered with other illogical examples— and then the parties argue as to whose are correct.

16. *Does losing your temper negatively influence the negotiation?*

The loss of temper sometimes negatively affects the process because, in "losing their cool," some negotiators forget their objectives and goals. And strong emotions are frequently a deterrent to creating alternatives and options. Yet there are circumstances in which negotiators lose their temper intentionally. The ploy works especially well for the individual who is generally perceived as calm, collected, and unflappable. When such a person flies off the handle, others sit up and take notice.

17. When reaching an impasse, is it better to call the negotiation to a halt and leave?

Almost never should you call the negotiation to a halt and walk out when an impasse is reached. (See chapter 6 on alternatives when at an impasse, and if these suggestions don't work then go ahead and walk out—remembering that you may have to eat crow and later return to the negotiating table.)

18. Should the first and/or final offer be made by your opponent?

This has been one of the most misunderstood questions in our survey. Many myths have been built up in the past about who ought to make the first or final offer. Our findings indicate that the negotiator with the greatest number of fallback positions can make the first offer; the one who has the greatest number of possible compromises may also make the final offer. Therefore, sometimes the opponent should make the first/final offer; sometimes you are better off doing so. However, always attempt to get something in return.

19. Do most individuals know when it is time to close a deal or end a negotiation?

Negotiators seldom know when to close a deal. Overwhelming evidence indicates that very many pass up a happy ending and are not aware of it. Further, as in sales, many negotiators talk themselves out of a settlement. The proper timing for a close is a very difficult thing to teach. Those who are successful at closing are usually the ones who recap and summarize so as to bring parties to well-timed common or mutual agreements. Although many negotiations are successful in spite of poor timing, the success ratio would be higher if parties cultivated a better sense of when to conclude.

20. Can negotiators read each other "like a book"?

Successful negotiators do often read each other like a book. It is a developed skill that many negotiators rely on and use constantly. Understanding how the other party is reacting to you is vitally important for sensing the flow and flavor of a negotiation. Being less aware or not reading someone's feelings can be disastrous. I find negotiators extremely conscious of the importance of reading the other person, and the portion of our seminar that covers nonverbal communication continues to be the most popular with our seminar attendees.

21. Is it true that the more dominant a negotiator is, the more effective he becomes?

Dominance seldom contributes to success in negotiations. In many cases, it leads to greater resistance and uncooperative behavior. The successful negotiator, instead of flexing his muscles, is resourceful in using other approaches in his attempt to get a settlement. Sophisticated negotiators do not make compromises because someone acts more dominant or forceful. They view negotiators who tend to use force as individuals who cannot handle stress or frustration. Our findings clearly reveal that the tougher the tactics, the tougher the resistance. Persuasiveness—not dominance—makes for a more effective negotiation.

22. Does the supportive negotiator tend to experience less conflict in negotiations?

Sometimes the negotiator who projects a supportive attitude toward his opposite experiences less conflict. However, because the process brings together parties who do have differences, a display of conflict is often healthy. Regardless of how cooperative or supportive you may be, conflict will probably have to be faced and handled. The positive factor with a supportive negotiator is that he encounters less resistance and hostility, especially when the support comes as a surprise. But even so, he must face up to the differences in outlook and position—and represent his own position well—if he is to be successful.

23. Is the use of levity effective?

The use of humor during especially difficult periods has often been effective. Levity, however, is not recommended for those who don't have a sense of timing. Telling a joke or a funny story at an inappropriate moment can sometimes lead to an explosion. If you haven't a natural sense of timing when it comes to wit and humor, it's best not to rely on levity to make or accentuate your point. In the end, you can be taught *how* to be funny, but not *when*.

24. Should compliments be used?

Complimenting the other party about how well prepared they were, how well they conducted the negotiation, etc., often gets good results. Premature compliments, on the other hand, are sometimes taken to be false and ingratiating. All negotiators, when a deal is consummated, like to feel they have been tough and fair and are respected. A little complimentary action goes a long way. Excessive amounts arouse suspicion.

25. Should opening statements and positions be emphatic?

Opening positions and demands often should be emphatic, to convey your commitment, dedication, and resolve to achieve objectives. Yet they should not be inflexible. There is a subtlety in making opening positions that are firm yet suggest the possibility of compromise. Most negotiators understand that "no" means "maybe" and "maybe" means "yes, try me harder," so don't be afraid of taking an initial hard position.

26. Does the amount of time spent in negotiating influence the outcome?

The amount of time spent often does influence the outcome of many negotiations. One of the persistent weaknesses that inexperienced negotiators display is their inability to deal with long negotiations. They tend to become impatient, to rush through, often making premature compromises. The more experienced person takes his time, knowing that when the settlement comes, time will have been a favorable factor. There is danger in equating time and value when a negotiation is prolonged merely for the sake of gaining time. In such instances, the outcome may not be as favorable, because in prolonging the process, the parties tend to belabor issues and develop stronger positions than originally intended. In other words, they dig in deeper and find it difficult to extract themselves. Historically, this has been a major problem in relations among nations. Positions become so entrenched that they become inflexible.

27. Do most negotiators enjoy stressful periods?

Although the negotiating process creates conflict and stress, negotiators seldom enjoy stress. They endure it and try to alleviate it. They have the ability to allow the temperature to rise without feeling in danger of getting burned. Harry Truman's statement about staying out of the kitchen applies to negotiators as well.

28. Is it easier to negotiate on the telephone?

Although thousands of individuals daily do so, negotiations on the phone are seldom effective. Good negotiators would rather deal face to face so that eye contact is possible. The greatest difficulty with telephone negotiating is the lack of nonverbal communication, which is so important to all negotiations. It is very difficult to get reenforcing feedback from the other person where there is no eye contact. For these reasons, we emphasize: Never negotiate on the phone when physical contact is possible.

29. When individuals say "That's not negotiable," should you believe them?

You should almost never believe someone who says an issue is not negotiable. Everything is subject to negotiation. What the person means is, "I don't want to discuss that issue today, but maybe tomorrow I will"; at other times he means, "I'm not willing to compromise in any way on that issue, but try me anyway," or, "You've hit a sensitive spot, lay off." However, we should always attempt to negotiate something the other person says is impossible. Don't take no for an answer; be persistent.

30. Are additional team negotiating members useful?

Often additional team members are very helpful. My feeling is that the optimum negotiating team consists of two members. That one additional person provides you with someone else who can note what is being communicated verbally and nonverbally—and with an additional mind to think and find alternatives. With more than two you increase the danger of a loss of direction, control, etc. The situation then may as often be one of negotiating within the team as of negotiating as a team with the opposition. The usefulness of the team is commensurate with the ability of the chief negotiator to utilize the members at appropriate times. Obviously, the longer individuals have negotiated together as a team, the more cohesive the group. See pages 88–89 for ways in which negotiators at times do not use team members effectively.

31. Should the "hard-nosed" approach be used?

Sometimes the "hard-nosed" approach should be used in outlining what position you've taken. This is particularly true in cases where the other party's role is to sell, influence, persuade, or motivate you. The hard-nosed approach is not as successful when you are the one who has to sell, influence, etc. I find that hard-nosed attitudes fall into three categories: (1) "No matter what you say, I'm not buying—save your breath"; (2) "No matter what you say, I'll appear as though I'm not buying"; (3) "What you say had better be convincing, good, logical, practical, and applicable." If you can distinguish between these categories, you'll find yourself better able to assess when to and when not to press your point. This is important for maximizing chances of success.

32. Is negotiating in your office an advantage to you?

When the venue of negotiating is a factor, it is sometimes in your favor to be meeting in your office or facility because: (1) You have ready access to records and other data; (2) you can easily call on other individuals for assistance; (3) you make the arrangements for seating, lunch breaks, etc.; (4) prolongation is easier when that is the tactic—visitors are usually more eager to get the negotiation over with and return home; (5) there can be a psychological advantage in a familiar setting where you can possibly tolerate more pressure and frustration.

33. Are negotiators truthful about what they "want"?

Negotiators seldom need what they originally ask for. That's another way of saying individuals ask for more things than they actually expect to get. Since most of us have high levels of expectation when we go into a negotiation, we tend to maximize our position in order to achieve the most. Remember Samuel Gompers' comment about what the goals of organized labor were? "More." We too attempt to get as much as we can and enjoy the process of paring down the other party as close to the need core as possible.

34. Do most negotiators listen?

Sometimes negotiators are good listeners, although it is a skill we should always exercise. In other chapters of this book I have emphasized the importance of listening and ways in which improvement is possible.

35. When individuals "walk out" of a negotiation, is it planned?

Often when negotiators walk out it is because it was planned beforehand or during a caucus. However, on some occasions, negotiations break down and one or both parties are ready to walk out as an emotional response.

Sometimes the level of anxiety and frustration becomes intolerable, and people do occasionally lose their tempers. When one party is out of emotional control and the other is not, a salvage may be possible. However, when one triggers the other and both flare up emotionally, a cooling period is required. The walkout sometimes provides that.

36. In general, are negotiators very creative?

Most successful negotiators are often very creative in developing alternatives. Those who are less successful seldom exercise other options and tend to stay stubbornly with one.

Winning the negotiation requires a wide range of aptitudes and skills—developing awareness, listening and observing, strategical planning and tactical maneuvering, a sense of timing, many other things. Now that you've reviewed these elements and become alert to the wide variety of ways in which creativity in achieving success can be stimulated, it is my hope that you will experience the satisfaction of success many times over.

I wish you good negotiating.

Index

Adaptability, 15–17
Adolescent negotiators, 11–14, 16
  intimidation and, 12–14
  return to "demand" strategy,
    12
  self-reliance and dependency,
    11
Adrenalin factor, 34–35
Adulthood, 14–21
  considering alternative situa-
    tions, 17–21
  either/or (instead of if/then),
    14–15
  patience and, 17
  smoothing of rough edges, 15–
    17
Agreement-in-principle, 50–52
  attempting to get, 98
Agreement-settlement, 141
All-or-none situation, 44
Alternatives
  to break a deadlock, 99–100
  considering, 17–21
  creative (or mutual), 58–60
  at an impasse, 94–105
  rejecting, 87–88

tactics for presenting the mes-
  sage, 19–21
American Broadcasting Company,
  66
Analysis, leverage, 127
Anxiety, 85
Art of Thinking, The (Dimmet),
  149
Ascent of Man, The (Bronowski),
  141–142
Assistance from others, 124
Association, 150–153
Attentiveness, 55–57
Attitudes, anticipating, 122–123
Awareness, 53, 62
  improving, 138–144

"Background music" (expression
  of stored feelings), 42–43
Behavior
  anticipating, 122–123
  starting positions, 136
Belief systems, 35–37
  that clash, 36–37
  complementary, 36
Bible, 61

Bit-by-bit tactic, 112–113
Brainstorming, 146–147
Breaking a deadlock, 96–105
  asking hypothetical question,
    100–101
  attempting agreement in prin-
    ciple, 98
  bridge-issue agreement, 98–99
  caucus, 97
  changing locations, 104
  changing the subject, 98
  diagram differences, 102
  discussing alternatives, 99–100
  doomsday tactic, 97
  by empathy, 101
  by expressing feelings, 97–98
  giving to get something, 102–
    103
  making strategic disclosures,
    100
  recap perspective, 97
  talking about past and future
    needs, 103
  trying a quick close, 101–102
  using past history and good
    association, 103–104
  walking out, 104–105
Bridge-issue agreement, 98–99
"Bridge issues," 45–46
Bronowski, Jacob, 141–142
Business negotiation, 21

Camp David meeting (1978), 45
Castro, Fidel, 75
Caucus, 97
Changing the subject, 98
Childhood, 2, 3–11, 16
  ability to read others, 9–10
  creative alternatives, 3–4
  and divide and conquer tactic,
    5–6
  honesty, 4–5
  knowing what children want,
    7–8
  persistence, 10–11
  timing, 6–7
  uninhibited trait, 8–9
Churchill, Winston, 102–103,
  143, 144
Cigarette smokers, 63
Climate stage, developing, 139–
  140

Company acquisition, 18
Complementary belief systems,
  36
Compromise, 30–32
  planning, 128
Compromise and fallback, 49–50
Concentration, 148–150
Conflict phase, 46–49
  skill development and, 140–141
Confrontation (either/or), dif-
  ference between negotiation
  (if/then) and, 15
Convergent association, 151
Cranshaw, Edward, 75
Creating needs, 27–28
Creative alternatives, 3–4
Creative Dreaming (Garfield),
  147
Creative potential, increasing,
  141–153
"Crib-type" negotiators, 1–2
Cuban missile crisis (1962), 66–
  75, 90

Deadlocks. *See* Breaking a dead-
  lock
Debate, confusing negotiation
  with, 84–85
De Bono, Edward, 4, 144
"Demand" strategy, 12
Developed visual aid, 131–132
Diagram differences, 102
Dimmet, Ernest, 149
Disclosure of information, badly
  handled, 80–81
Divergent association, 151
Divide and conquer tactic (child-
  negotiator), 5–6
Doomsday tactic, 97, 117–118
"Do you really want our busi-
  ness?" tactic, 116
Dreams, creativity in, 147

Effective negotiators, characteristics of, 52–57
  attentiveness, 55–57
  awareness, 53
  flexibility, 54–55
  patience, 52–54
Ego needs, 29–30
Einstein, Albert, 148
Either/or situations, 14–15

Emerson, Ralph Waldo, 60
Emotions, 16, 61
Empathy, giving or getting, 101

Fallback and compromise, 49–50
Fallback positions, planning, 128
Fay, Dr. Allen, 148
Feelings, 16, 61
    not disclosing, 88
    expressing, 97–98
"Fight or flight" situation, 64
Fingertips, 65
Fishing, 119–120
Flesch, Rudolph, 58
Flexibility, 54–55
Frost, Robert, 150
Frustration under control, 17
Funny money tactic, 118
Future needs, talking about, 103

Garfield, Patricia, 147
Garner, James, 24–25
Gestures, 61
Giving, to get something, 102–103
Good association, using, 103–104
Good guy-bad guy ploy, 108–109
Gordon, William J., 146–147
Greater rewards tactic, 109–110
Group creativity, 146–147

Hart, B.H. Liddell, 145–146
Harvey (motion picture), 49
Hidden communication, 60–65
    types of, 61
Hitler, Adolf, 92
Honesty, 4–5
Hubbard, Frank McKinney, 71
Hypothetical question, 100–101

"I care" approach, 19
"I don't have the authority"
    ploy, 111–112
"I don't know what's wrong, but
    unless things change"
    ultimatum, 20
If/then situations, 14–15
"I have a friend" message, 19
"I know something is wrong"
    tactic, 19
"I may be wrong" gambit, 19
Imagination, skill development
    and, 144–145

Impasse, 94–105
    breaking deadlocks, 96–105
    U.S. Embassy in Moscow case,
        94–96
Indirect approaches, alertness to,
    145–146
Infancy, 1–2
Inspector General, The (motion
    picture), 65
International conflicts, 37
Intimidation, 130
    adolescent, 12–14
Intra-organization negotiating,
    problems in, 89–93
Invoking the competition tactic,
    110–111
Issues
    analysis of, 123–124
    definition of, 43–46
    selecting the first to be dis-
        cussed, 44–46
"It's not industry practice"
    tactic, 116–117
"It's not standard!" ploy, 113

Juxtaposition, skill development
    and, 142–144

Kaye, Danny, 65
Kennedy, John F., 74
Kennedy, Robert F., 67–68, 70,
    71, 72, 75
"Kill them with kindness" strat-
    egy, 20–21
Khruschchev, Nikita, 73, 74, 75
Khrushchev Remembers (Cran-
    shaw), 75

Lateral thinking, 4
Leaving messages around, 21
Leverage, 24–27
    providing, 24–25
Leverage analysis, 26–27, 127
Life needs, 29
Locations, changing, 104

Making Things Better by Making
    Them Worse (Fay), 148
Maslow, Abraham, 28
Maximizing a position, 23–24
Memory, 150
"Missiles of October, The" (TV
    documentary), 66–67

Mistakes, 76–93
  badly handled disclosures of
    information, 80–81
  confusing negotiation with
    debate, 84–85
  in intra-organization negotiat-
    ing, 89–93
  mismanaging presentation of
    issues, 82–83
  misuse of team members, 89
  not disclosing feelings, 88–89
  overreacting to stress, 85–87
  poor listening, 76–77
  poor use of questions, 76–80
  rejecting alternatives, 87–88
Momentum, 32–33
Moses, 61
Multiple answers, skill develop-
    ment and, 144

Needs (how to sell and/or create),
    22–37
  adrenalin factor in, 34–35
  belief system, 35–37
  bringing to the surface, 27–28
  compromise, 30–32
  leverage, providing, 24–25
  leverage analysis, 26–27
  maximizing position, 23–24
  momentum, 32–33
  objectives, 30
  satisfaction, 22
  timing, 33–34
  variety of, 28–30
Negotiation process
  adolescent period, 11–14, 16
  adulthood, 14–21
  case study (Cuban missile
    crisis), 66–75, 90
  childhood, 2, 3–11, 16
  developing skills, 138–153
  impasse, 94–105
  of infants, 1–2
  introduction to, ix–xi
  meaning of, 22–37
  mistakes, 76–93
  planning, 121–137
  profile questionnaire response,
    154–171
  reasons for, 22–23
  ritual, 38–65
  skills questionnaire, xii–xiii
  strategy and tactics, 106–120

New Think (de Bono), 142

Objectives, 30
  analysis of, 123–124
Opposite approach, using, 147–
    148
Outside assistance, 124
Overkill, 65

Past history, using, 103–104
Past needs, talking about, 103
Patience, 53–54
  as frustration under control, 17
Persistence, child's, 10–11
Peter, Dr. Laurence J., 153
Peter's Quotations, 153
Planning, 121–137
  analysis of objectives and
    issues, 123–124
  anticipation of attitudes and
    behavior, 122–123
  compromises and fallback
    positions, 128
  getting the negotiations started,
    134–137
  leverage analysis, 127
  outside assistance, 124
  post-negotiation analysis, 133–
    134
  preparation for, 121–122
  psychological factors, 128–130
  strategies and tactics, 126–127
  use of visual aids, 131–133
Plomer, William, 153
PO: Beyond Yes and No
    (de Bono), 142
Poor listening, 76–77
Poor use of questions, 76–80
Post-negotiation analysis, 133–
    134
Post-settlement, 52
Posture, 61–62
Practical Thinking (de Bono),
    142
Prepared visual aids, 131
Presentation of issues, misman-
    aging, 82–83
Profile questionnaire response,
    154–171
Psychological factors, planning,
    128–130
Pupil-to-mentor approach, 13

Questions, poor use of, 76–80
Quick-close ploy, 119
Quick close, trying, 101–102

Reading others intuitively, 9–10
Recap perspective, 97
Rejecting alternatives, mistake
   of, 87–88
Reverse psychology, 147–148
Ritual, 38–65
   agreement-in-principle, 50–52
   "background music," 42–43
   benchmarks of success, 57–58
   conflict phase, 46–49
   creative (or mutual) alterna-
     tives, 58–60
   definition of issues, 43–46
   effective characteristics, 52–57
   fallback and compromise, 49–
     50
   general overview, 40–41
   hidden communication, 60–65
   introductory phase, 39–40
   post-settlement, 52
Rough edges, smoothing, 15–17

Self-admonishment, 114
Self-change (to improve the
   situation), 21
Self-deprivation, 2
Self-discipline, 60
Self-injury, 2
Self-reliance and dependency,
   duality of, 11
Self-respect, 29
"Selling" persuasion, 23
Settlement phase, 50–52
Shakespeare, William, 55
Silence, 64
Skills, developing, 138–153
   awareness, 138–144
   creative potential, 141–153
Skills questionnaire, xii–xiii
Starting positions, 134–137
   behavior and, 136
Stewart, Jimmy, 49
Strategic disclosures, 100
Strategy (Hart), 145–146
Strategy and tactics, 106–120
   bit-by-bit, 112–113
   doomsday, 117–118
   "do you really want our busi-
     ness?," 116

fishing, 119–120
   funny money, 118
   good guy-bad guy, 108–112
   "it's not industry practice,"
     116–117
   "it's not standard," 113
   planning, 126–127
   quick close, 119
   self-admonishment, 114
   undermining, 107–108
   wet noodle, 114
   "what could be wrong," 115–
     116
Stress, overreacting to, 85–87
Stroke-and-get tactic, 2–3
Support Your Local Sheriff?
   (motion picture), 24–25
Svevo, Italo, 150
Synectics (Gordon), 146–147

Team members, misuse of, 89
Team negotiation, planning com-
   position of, 125–126
Thirteen Days (Kennedy), 67–68,
   70, 71, 72, 75
Timing factor, 33–34
Toe-up message, 63–64
Tolerance, 16

Undermining tactic, 107–108
Uninhibited trait, 8–9
United Nations, 70
U.S. Embassy in Moscow case,
   94–96
Use of Lateral Thinking, The
   (de Bono), 142, 144

Vietnam War, 69
Visual aids, use of, 131–133
Visualization of how to close
   agreement, 102

Walking out, 104–105
Washington, George, 5
We're the greatest tactic, 109
Wet noodle tactic, 114–115
"What could be wrong?" ploy,
   115–116
"When are you . . .?" inquiry, 20
"Why don't you" overture, 19
Wizard of Oz, The, 33
"Would you talk to" strategy,
   19–20